THE OFFICIAL

Tottenham Hotspur

FANS' GUIDE

THIS IS A CARLTON BOOK

This edition published in 1997

10 9 8 7 6 5 4 3 2 1

Produced Under Licence From Tottenham Hotspur Plc.

Copyright © 1997 Carlton Books Limited and
Tottenham Hotspur Football Club Plc.

The Club Badge and Shield and the words "Tottenham Hotspur" and
"Spurs" are registered trademarks of Tottenham Hotspur Plc.

A CIP catalogue record for this book is available from the British Library

ISBN 1 85868 411 0

Project Editor: Martin Corteel
Project art direction: Paul Messam
Production: Garry Lewis and Sarah Schuman
Picture research: Victoria Walker
Designed by Jim Stanton

Author's acknowledgements
The author would like to thank Tottenham's club historian Andy Porter
for his invaluable assistance, Stefano Bozzi, Adrian Curtis, Conrad
Leach, Mark McGuinness, Charlene Sales and all at Teamwork Sports
Agency. He would also like to thank his father, Sid, for inspiring this
obsession and his wife, Bernadette, for tolerating it.

Printed in Italy

THE OFFICIAL
Tottenham Hotspur

FANS' GUIDE

THE STORY OF
THE PREMIER LEAGUE YEARS

GERRY COX

CARLTON

Contents

Allan Nielsen vs. Manchester Utd in August 1997

Gerry Francis, thoughtful, in July 1995

The Park Lane South Stand at White Hart Lane

Introduction

The first five years of Tottenham's time in the Premiership have been as notable for events off the field as on it. Spurs have not won a trophy in that time, but they have made headlines consistently during that period, for all sorts of reasons.

As befits the club's tradition as the great entertainers of English football, they have given fans and critics alike plenty of food for thought since 1992.

Controversy has never been far away, an inevitability, perhaps, given the club's size and stature in the game.

There have been court cases, sackings, a European ban, a points deduction and expulsion from the FA Cup, although the last three were all overturned. Big names have come and gone, the team has flirted with relegation and success, and White Hart Lane has undergone major redevelopment in the past five years. And all the time, Tottenham Hotspur plc has been gradually hauling itself back into a position of strength.

When the brave new world of Premier League football dawned in 1992, Spurs were still clawing their way back from the brink of bankruptcy. It is fair to say that they started life in the Premiership at a major financial disadvantage, having almost gone under barely 12 months earlier.

That Spurs are back in business is a testament to the shrewdness and business sense of Chairman Alan Sugar and Chief Executive Claude Littner, who have turned round a deficit of almost £20 million so that the club are now in a position to spend that sort of money in the transfer market without over-reaching themselves.

While most supporters appreciate that fact, they are naturally impatient for success on the field. Five years is a long time to go without a trophy for a club with Tottenham's traditions. Yet fans should remember that the club's history has been punctuated by long barren periods in the past, and no amount of money can guarantee success.

Tottenham were the first club to import foreign superstars when Keith Burkinshaw signed World Cup winners Ossie Ardiles and Ricky Villa in 1978. More recently, they led the wave of world-class superstars playing in the Premiership when they signed Jürgen Klinsmann, Ilie Dumitrescu and Gica Popescu in 1994.

However, they have continued the tried and trusted method of nurturing their own talent — a policy that has paid handsome dividends for Manchester United in the past few years.

For every big-name signing like David Ginola and Chris Armstrong there has been an outstanding youngster coming through the ranks, as shown by the emergence of Sol Campbell, Nick Barmby and Ian Walker as eventual England internationals. There is a new generation of talented youngsters waiting to come though, and the future at White Hart Lane is full of promise. But here we concentrate on what has gone before – the highs, the lows, and everything in between.

This book has everything for today's Spurs supporter; player profiles, great games and a complete statistical breakdown of the past five seasons. The past has not been forgotten, and there are chapters on the club's history before 1992 and traditions in the cups and in Europe.

It is essential reading for any Spurs fan and gives a fascinating insight into what makes Tottenham Hotspur a special club in the hearts of so many people.

Les Ferdinand, Tottenham's big-name summer signing of 1997, went straight into action

Chapter 1

The History of Spurs

Tottenham's history is full of ups and downs, triumphs and defeats, and heartbreak. But most of all it is about glory, style and a certain way of playing the game.

If you know your history...

It is fitting that one of the greatest tales in the history of English football should have been influenced by that master story-teller, Shakespeare. Admittedly the Bard pre-dated the club's formation by more than 200 years, but it was his character Harry Hotspur who inspired the small group of North London schoolboys who founded the club.

Legend has it that in 1882 a group of a dozen or so teenagers gathered under a gas lamp opposite what is now the club shop at the Park Lane end of the ground. They had started the Hotspur Cricket Club two years earlier and wanted to form a football club to play throughout the winter months.

Harry Hotspur was in fact Sir Henry Percy, teenage son of the Earl of Northumberland in the 15th Century. His gallant adventures captured the imagination of these local grammar school boys, especially as the Percy family owned large parts of north London. The local area was even known as Northumberland Park.

So it was that they chose Hotspur as their patron and named their new club after him. The Hotspur Football Club, which was changed to Tottenham Hotspur two years later in 1884, to avoid confusion with London Hotspur, was formally instituted on September 5, 1882, with 11 founder-members paying subscriptions.

Their first game was on September 30, 1882, a 2–0 defeat against the Radicals, but their first recorded game was an 8–1 defeat by local rivals Latymer of Edmonton in January 1883. Later that year the club came under the patronage of the local YMCA, moving a mile down the road to play at Tottenham Marshes.

Their first competitive game came in 1885, when they defeated St Albans 5–2 in the London Association Cup, before losing 8–0 to the Casuals. By this time Spurs had changed from their original colours of all-blue to blue and white, although there were to be combinations of red and blue and chocolate and gold before they settled on their famous navy and white strip in 1898.

They were still playing on the Marshes, but in 1888 the club found a private pitch for hire in Northumberland Park. The rent was £17 per annum but they offset that by charging an admission price of threepence per game.

Having moved quickly from being a group of schoolboys playing friendly matches to a proper club watched by thousands, they joined the burgeoning Football Association in 1889, although they were still amateur and unable to play in an organized league.

A move to professionalism was hastened by an

incident in 1893 concerning left-winger Ernie Payne, who had moved to Spurs from Fulham. When he discovered his kit was missing on the morning of his first game, Payne was given ten shillings to buy a new pair of boots.

Fulham heard about this and complained to the London FA, who found Spurs guilty of breaching their strict rules concerning financial payments. Spurs were suspended for a fortnight but the incident brought them more publicity and bigger crowds. They eventually turned professional in 1895 and joined the new Southern League, having been turned down by the Football League.

The new professional era meant big changes, and in 1898 the club became a limited company. The visit of South Londoners Woolwich Arsenal soon afterwards attracted a record crowd of 14,000 to Northumberland Park, which was now. clearly too small.

The directors found a plot of land off Tottenham High Road which had previously been used as a market garden, just a few yards from where the club had originally been founded. The site was next to the White Hart pub which was owned by Charrington's brewery, who were keen to provide extra custom for the pub. They agreed to lease the site to Spurs on the understanding that the club would guarantee 1,000 spectators for first-team games and 500 for reserve matches.

Stands were imported from Northumberland Park and the new 30,000-capacity ground was officially opened with a resounding 4–1 win over Notts County in 1899. Names suggested for the stadium included Gilpin Park and Percy Park, but it eventually became known as White Hart Lane.

Within a year, Spurs had won the Southern League. Led by Scottish player-manager John Cameron and Welsh captain Jack Jones, they won 20 and drew four of their 28 games to win the title.

The club was in profit, the reserve team were also flourishing and Spurs were on the up. Everything was in place for a successful club. All that was needed to complete the picture was that first trophy.

The 1901 FA Cup-winners. Sandy Brown (front row, centre) scored 15 goals that season – still a record

The first great side

The fact that Spurs won the most famous cup competition of all while still in the Southern League is remarkable enough, but for them to do so less than 20 years after being founded by a group of schoolboys looking for a Saturday afternoon kick–about is even more astonishing.

Tottenham's FA Cup triumph over Sheffield United in 1901 was the first and only victory by a non-League club since the Football League's formation in 1888. It was also the only FA Cup win by a professional Southern side before Spurs repeated the feat 20 years later. But Spurs were no longer made up of Londoners, despite being called "The Flower of the South" in the newspapers.

The most locally-born member of their FA Cup-winning team in 1901 was Tom Morris, who came from Grantham in Lincolnshire – in the East Midlands! The northern influence was largely due to John Cameron, who had played for Scotland, Queen's Park and Everton. At the time, English football was dominated by the powerful professional clubs from the Midlands, North and Scotland. Any teams from south of Birmingham were regarded as the original "Southern Softies".

Cameron assembled a team of Scots, Irish and Welshmen complemented by Northerners, not one of them born within 100 miles of White Hart Lane. But Cameron's men were preparing to take on and beat all comers. They achieved this with that historic FA Cup

victory over Sheffield United in 1901 which drew a world-record crowd of 114,815 (For more details of the 1901 FA Cup win see Chapter 4 – Up for the Cup).

But just as great things appeared to be on the horizon, Tottenham's fortunes began to decline. Centre-forward Sandy Brown left for Middlesbrough after a remarkable 12 months at Spurs, scoring 15 goals in that Cup run – still a record.

His replacement was one of the first Greats of English football. Vivian Woodward was among the most famous amateurs of his era, captaining England to their Olympic successes of 1908 and 1912 (see Box 1) Woodward scored Tottenham's first goal in League football after they were elected in 1908. Spurs had grown disenchanted with the Southern League and saw other London clubs such as Chelsea, Clapton Orient and Fulham joining the Football League.

Spurs, along with QPR and Bradford Park Avenue, announced their intention to apply for membership of the Football League, a move that had them expelled from the Southern League in April 1908.

Their application to join the League did not go smoothly, however, as they ended fifth behind Grimsby, Chesterfield, Bradford PA and Lincoln in the voting. It looked like they might have to play friendlies again, but then Stoke decided to resign from the League. A special ballot was held and Spurs tied with Lincoln twice before being voted into the League by the management committee.

Spurs won promotion to the first division at the first attempt but over the next few seasons were less

Spurs vs. Blackburn, White Hart Lane, 1911. Robinson saves Sandy Young's shot

Tottenham parade their second FA Cup in 1921 after beating Wolves 1–0 in the final at Stamford Bridge. It would be 30 years – the longest barren spell in Spurs' history – before their next trophy

successful as they battled against relegation. At the end of the 1914–15 season Spurs finished bottom, but the League was then suspended for four years because of the First World War and White Hart Lane was taken over for the manufacture of gas-masks.

When the war ended and League football resumed in 1919, it was decided to increase the size of the first division to 22 clubs. Normally it would have meant keeping the bottom two clubs, Spurs and Chelsea, and electing two more from the second division.

But after a controversial move by the management committee, Spurs had to contest a vote with six other clubs, coming second to Arsenal (who had finished only fifth in the second division) who therefore leapfrogged over higher-placed teams to take Tottenham's place (See Chapter 11 – The North London Derby).

The Gunners have been in the top flight ever since, but as any Spurs fan who knows their history will tell you, they never won promotion in the first place. Spurs took revenge by romping to the second-division title,

scoring 102 goals and amassing 70 points, a new League record. They were back in the first division and determined to make a name for themselves.

Vivian Woodward

Vivian Woodward was the first great player in Tottenham's history and a true Corinthian. An architect by profession, he joined Spurs from Chelmsford in 1901 and even became a director before surprisingly resigning in 1909 after scoring 75 goals in 151 games. He later joined Chelsea and became a director at Stamford Bridge. He played six times for the England and UK amateur sides, captaining England to Olympic gold in 1908 and 1912. Woodward also played in 23 internationals and scored 29 goals – an England record until Tom Finney overtook it in 1958.

Rise and fall between the Wars

The year is 1920, and no Southern side had tasted success since Tottenham's famous FA Cup win of 1901. The next two decades saw a return to domination by the Northern and Midlands clubs. Under manager Peter McWilliam, Spurs were about to change that.

Like John Cameron before him, McWilliam had been a Scottish international with an illustrious playing career before turning to management with Spurs in 1912. He put together a skilful, attacking side which stormed to the second-division title in 1920, and won the FA Cup the following year.

Led by long-serving captain Arthur Grimsdell and with the goals of Bert Bliss, Jimmy Banks and Jimmy Seed, Spurs were favourites to win the final against Wolves at Stamford Bridge and scored the game's only goal, when local hero Jimmy Dimmock shot home after 54 minutes to seal victory.

The following year Spurs lost in the semi-final to Preston but confirmed their growing status as the best club in Southern England by finishing as runners-up to Liverpool in the League, their highest placing and the best ever by a side from the South. But like the 1901 side, just when it seemed that things were about to take off, Spurs suddenly went into decline. They finished no higher than 12th in the next five years, and after Peter McWilliam resigned in February 1927 because of a wrangle over wages, Spurs were relegated the following season in bizarre circumstances.

Jimmy Seed (see box) had lost his place through injury to Welshman Eugene "Taffy" O'Callaghan. Former inside-forward Billy Minter had taken over from McWilliam as manager and decided to sell Seed to Sheffield Wednesday, who were five points adrift at the bottom of the table. With Seed inspiring them, they picked up and beat mid-table Spurs twice over Easter. Seed scored in each game.

Spurs finished their games earlier than other teams and went on tour to Holland, still well above the relegation zone. When they returned they found they had

The remarkable Jimmy Seed leads Spurs into combat. He helped Spurs win the FA Cup in 1921, led Sheffield Wednesday to two League Championships and, as manager of Charlton, steered them to their 1947 FA Cup victory

Jimmy Seed

Tottenham's most remarkable character in the pre-war years was a man called Jimmy Seed. Released by Sunderland after being gassed in the First World War, he was signed by Spurs from Mid-Rhondda in 1920. The following year he played a key part in their FA Cup success. After losing his place through injury in 1928 he was sold to Sheffield Wednesday, who were bottom of the League at the time. He helped them stay up as Spurs were relegated, then led them to the Championship for the next two seasons. He later became a highly successful manager of Charlton, taking them to two FA Cup finals, and a director of Millwall.

been relegated in one of the closest final League tables ever. Seven clubs finished with one point more than them, and even fourth-placed Derby had only six points more.

Spurs remained in the second division until 1933, by which time Percy Smith had taken over from Minter as manager. Smith brought in Ted Harper from Sheffield Wednesday and the centre-forward repaid him with goals, scoring 36 in one season, a club record until Jimmy Greaves beat it almost 30 years later.

Willie Hall was another inspired signing. The little inside-forward was not a prolific goalscorer but set a remarkable record when he hit five goals in one game – all in the space of 28 minutes – for England against Ireland, a feat that has never been bettered.

Tottenham's promotion season of 1932 was helped by the forward line of George Hunt, Willie Evans and Taffy O'Callaghan scoring 75 goals between them. The same three continued to score goals in the first division as Spurs finished third, but they were relegated again the following season and spent the remaining pre-war years in the second division.

One high point during this black period was an FA cup sixth-round tie with Sunderland that drew 75,038 to White Hart Lane, still a club record. Smith gave way to manager Jack Tresadern, who only lasted three seasons before Peter McWilliam was brought back. The former manager had just one season before the Second World War started, but he made a significant step in bringing through youngsters from Northfleet, Tottenham's nursery club. The rewards were to be reaped a decade later.

Push and run

Arthur Rowe's career as both player and manager with Spurs was punctuated by injury and illness, yet he became the club's most successful manager until Bill Nicholson in the 1960s, and still remains one of the most influential figures in Tottenham history.

Rowe was a Spurs man through and though. Born locally, his earliest memories were of watching Tottenham at White Hart Lane. He was a graduate of the Northfleet nursery, the Kent club where Spurs sent young players to get valuable experience, and signed professional terms at 20.

An attacking centre-half, he made his debut in 1931 and was a key member of the promotion-winning side in 1933, winning his only England cap the same year. But injury cut short his career and in 1938 he moved to Hungary to study coaching methods. He was all set to become the national coach before the Second World War forced him to return to his native England, where he continued to develop his ideas.

After winning the Southern League with Chelmsford City, he was offered the Spurs job when former Arsenal winger Joe Hulme left after three unsuccessful post-war seasons.

Rowe had always been a deep tactical thinker

As a manager Arthur Rowe (pictured in action against West Ham in 1935) transformed Spurs' tactics to help them win the League in 1950–51

about the game but his maxim was straightforward: "Make it simple, make it quick." His tactics were based on short passing and movement between players at speed, a stark contrast to the long ball game prevalent in England.

What became known as "push and run" was no more than the sort of passing and movement we take for granted from the world's best sides today, but in post-war Britain it was revolutionary.

Rowe's experiences in Hungary tutored him in a Continental style and he was fortunate to inherit a group of players, including Eddie Baily and Welsh captain Ron Burgess, who were able to carry it out to stunning effect.

Like all great sides, Tottenham's first line of attack was in defence, where legendary keeper Ted Ditchburn astonished English crowds by rolling the ball out to his defenders, notably Alf Ramsey and Bill Nicholson. It is perhaps no coincidence that those two went on to become the greatest English managers of their era, possibly of all time. They were key components of a side that played with style, intelligence and fluidity, devastatingly effective as well as beautiful to watch.

Not surprisingly, they took the second division by storm in 1949–50, a run of 22 games without defeat giving them an unassailable lead by January. The crowds flocked to watch this new wonder-team and White Hart Lane averaged almost 55,000 per game, higher than the First Division's best, Arsenal, with an average gate of 51,000.

More than 1.5 million fans watched the super Spurs at White Hart Lane that season, easily a club record, and they were rewarded with thrilling displays and a feeling that something exciting was on the way. They were not to be disappointed.

The 1950–51 season got off to an inauspicious start with a 4–1 home defeat by Blackpool, but doubts were soon eased when they won by the same score at Bolton a few days later. They really hit top form with a burst of eight straight wins that took them to the top by November. Spurs swept all before them, especially at home, beating Stoke 6–1, thumping League champions Portsmouth 5–1 and humiliating Newcastle 7–0.

They finally won the title by three points from Manchester United, their first League Championship and a thrilling end to a 30-year wait for honours.

But once again success was to be short-lived. United reversed the positions at the top the following season, and Spurs had to settle for the runners'-up

Tottenham's first League Championship-winning side, in 1950–51. Back row, first left is Alf Ramsey, who went on to lead England to the 1966 World Cup triumph. Next to him is Bill Nicholson, who became Tottenham's most successful manager

spot. In 1952–53, the players were beginning to show their age and opposing managers were learning how to counter Tottenham's style.

They reached the FA Cup semi-final to face Blackpool, a repeat of five years earlier, but a disastrous attempted back-pass from Ramsey in the closing seconds allowed Jimmy Mudie to score the winner.

Spurs struggled for the next two seasons and Rowe's health suffered. When he had a breakdown, his assistant Jimmy Anderson was asked to take over. Anderson had been at the club almost 50 years and was seen as a stop-gap while coach Bill Nicholson was being groomed for management. Even so, Anderson took Spurs to another FA Cup semi-final in 1956, where they lost to Manchester City, and more importantly helped lay the foundations for what was to become indisputably one of the greatest club sides in the history of the game.

Danny Blanchflower

Danny Blanchflower will always be remembered as captain of Bill Nicholson's double-winning side, but he was one of Arthur Rowe's last signings at a record £30,000 from Aston Villa in 1954. A great passer and thinker, Blanchflower could turn a game with one flash of inspiration.

He started his career in Northern Ireland with Glentoran before joining Barnsley and then Villa. But it was at Spurs that he had his greatest days, voted Footballer of the Year twice. He also captained Northern Ireland to the World Cup quarter-final in 1958. After retiring in 1964 he became a journalist, had a short spell as manager of Chelsea and Northern Ireland and died in 1993, shortly after Rowe.

The Double

No one could dream of a better start in management than the one that greeted Bill Nicholson. Taking over from Jimmy Anderson on the morning of Saturday October 11, 1958, Nicholson promptly saw the first side he sent out hammer Everton 10–4 a few hours later.

It is still the highest score in a first-division match this century, and the enigmatic Tommy Harmer had the game of his life. To Spurs fans it was a sign of great things to come – or was it? Results soon returned to normal with more defeats than wins, and Spurs narrowly escaped relegation. But Nicholson was slowly assembling a side to beat the world.

He already had his ace card in Blanchflower, and to

The great double-winning side of 1960–61. Spurs became the first side this century to win both the League Championship and the FA Cup in one season, a feat only ever matched by Arsenal, Liverpool and Manchester United

complement his touch and vision Nicholson added Dave Mackay. A tough-tackling, skilful Scot with a heart the size of a lion's, Mackay was the sort of player who would today be called the complete midfielder. Another Scot, Bill Brown, replaced Ted Ditchburn in goal after the legendary keeper retired having set a club record of 452 appearances. Under Anderson, barnstorming centre-forward Bobby Smith had been brought in from Chelsea, Welsh winger Cliff Jones was signed from Swansea for a British record fee of £35,000 and big Maurice Norman arrived from Norwich.

Spurs started the 1959–60 season with an unbeaten run of 12 games but blew their title chances at Easter and ended third. Ironically their last defeat, which ulti-

mately cost them the title, was against Chelsea, whose goalscorer was a teenage Jimmy Greaves (see box).

But Blanchflower was convinced Spurs could do the double, and they certainly started the season as if they meant business – 11 straight wins, still a record, and 16 games unbeaten from the start. In all, they won an unprecedented 31 games that season to gain a record-equalling 66 points, scoring 115 goals.

Spurs sealed the Championship with three games to spare by beating Sheffield Wednesday, just as they had done in 1951, and then concentrated on the second leg of the double – the FA Cup (See Chapter Four – Up for the Cup). If the 2–0 win over Leicester in the final was not a particularly entertaining spectacle, the occasion certainly was, as Spurs entered the record books alongside Preston and Aston Villa as double-winners –the first club to achieve the feat this century.

In November 1961 Nicholson brought Greaves back from Milan for a British record fee of £99,999. The unusual sum was specified to avoid making Greaves Britain's first £100,000 player, although there was no question of him failing to cope with the burden of expectation. He scored a hat-trick on his debut, against Blackpool and went on to become the club's record scorer, hitting 266 goals in 380 games for Spurs.

Spurs came within an ace of repeating their double, retaining the FA Cup by beating Burnley 3–1 but losing out to Ipswich – managed by Alf Ramsey – in the League. They also went close in the European Cup, reaching the semi-final before going out controversially (see Chapter Three – Spurs in Europe).

The following year they finished runners-up to Manchester United, but there was consolation when Terry Dyson inspired Spurs to a 5–1 victory over Atletico Madrid in the European Cup-winners' Cup final in Rotterdam (see Chapter Three – Spurs in Europe). It was another record for Spurs as they became the first British team to lift a European trophy.

But it was also the beginning of the end for the double side. Over the following two years, Smith was sold to Brighton, Blanchflower and Medwin had to retire through injury and Mackay broke his left leg twice, keeping him out for 18 months.

But most tragic of all was the death of John White, struck by lightning as he sheltered under a tree while out playing golf. The skilful Scotsman was only 26 and at the peak of his career, and his death was a devastating blow. Nicholson had lost the heart of his side and had to start again. In came Alan Gilzean and Jimmy Robertson from Scotland, Mike England from Wales

(Left) Jimmy Greaves hits home against Arsenal... in nine years at Spurs he set a club record of 266 goals (Above) Bill Nicholson and his assistant and former team-mate Eddie Baily

and young goalkeeper Pat Jennings from Northern Ireland. Londoners Alan Mullery and Terry Venables were signed as well as left-back Cyril Knowles from Middlesbrough. Youngsters Joe Kinnear and Phil Beal rose through the ranks, and Spurs beat Chelsea to win the FA Cup in 1967.

The following year saw the arrival of Martin Chivers from Southampton for a British record £125,000, but he suffered a serious knee injury soon afterwards. By the time he was fully fit again Greaves had gone, in an exchange deal that brought Martin Peters from West Ham for a new British record of £200,000.

It was a controversial move, and many fans never forgave Peters for replacing the legendary Greaves. But it paid off for Nicholson, as Spurs enjoyed three years of success. Chivers inspired them to their first League Cup triumph, over Aston Villa in 1971 (see Chapter Four, Up for the Cup) and they repeated that success by beating Norwich two years later.

There was also further success in Europe, with Alan Mullery returning from a loan spell at Fulham to seal the club's first UEFA Cup triumph in a two-legged final against Wolves in 1972 making them the first British club to win two European trophies (see Chapter Three – Spurs in Europe).

They lost to Liverpool on away goals in the semi-final the following year, but reached the final again in 1974. That final against Feyenoord, however, was the beginning of the end for Nicholson. Having conceded a late equalizer to the Dutch at home, Spurs had everything to do in the away leg. Their subsequent 2–0 defeat was overshadowed by disgraceful scenes of hooliganism in Rotterdam, with Nicholson having to appeal for calm at half-time. Spurs not only lost their first-ever final, but were banned from Europe by UEFA.

When they started the following season with four straight defeats, their worst start for 62 years, Nicholson resigned. He'd intended to go out at the top if Spurs had beaten Feyenoord a few months earlier, but had changed his mind. Now it was final: the greatest single figure in Tottenham's history and one of the most successful managers in the history of English football had left White Hart Lane after 38 years. It was the end of an era, and the start of even bleaker days for Spurs.

Jimmy Greaves

Jimmy Greaves was simply the greatest goalscorer in the history of Tottenham and post-war England. His strength was his speed and anticipation in the penalty box, and he set goalscoring records galore.

Starting with Chelsea, he became the youngest player to score 100 goals and then 200 goals. An ill-fated move to AC Milan soon ended when Spurs signed him for £99,999 in 1961 and he helped Spurs win two FA Cups and the Cup-winners' Cup.

He scored 44 goals in 57 games for England but Alf Ramsey left him out of the 1966 World Cup final, a decision that devastated Greaves. He eventually retired shortly after moving to West Ham in 1970 in exchange for Martin Peters, and is now a successful TV and newspaper personality.

Life after Nicholson

Replacing a legend like Bill Nicholson was never going to be easy, but when you are a former Arsenal captain it is nigh-on impossible. Terry Neill was given the unenviable task of trying to win over fans who were naturally sceptical about a man who had spent the majority of his playing career with their bitter rivals.

Nicholson's own choice was Blanchflower, and he discussed the job with him, but the board did not consult their former manager and were unhappy that the forceful Irishman had spent the previous decade as a journalist.

Instead they appointed Neill, only 32 at the time, with four modest years as player-manager of Hull. His first moves were to clear out the old guard and give youth a chance. But Spurs struggled with the changes and ended the season needing to beat Leeds in their final game to avoid relegation.

They won 4–2 to survive, and the following season finished in ninth place. A young midfielder called Glenn Hoddle scored a spectacular goal on his full debut and gave supporters a glimpse of his precocious talent. But Neill fell out with the board and resigned in June 1976. Three weeks later he was appointed manager of Arsenal, whom he subsequently led to three FA Cup finals and a Cup-winners' Cup final.

Neill's successor was his former assistant Keith Burkinshaw, a down-to-earth Yorkshireman like Nicholson, who was highly regarded as a coach. His first season in charge was a disaster – Spurs were relegated for the first time in 40 years. Burkinshaw then made a rod for his own back when he sold Spurs legend Pat Jennings – to Arsenal!

Jennings was 31, in the prime of his career and the best goalkeeper in Britain. He had just been voted Footballer of the Year and Player of the Year in successive seasons, beaten Ted Ditchburn's record for Spurs appearances and become Northern Ireland's most-capped player. But Burkinshaw thought his best days were behind him, a decision he came to regret, as Jennings had a highly successful career at Highbury before setting a new world record for international caps and eventually returning to Spurs in 1986 as goalkeeping cover. He is now employed at the club as goalkeeping coach.

Spurs scored freely in the second division, including a 9–0 win over Bristol Rovers with debutante Colin Lee scoring four times. In the end, however, they needed a point from their final game of the season to ensure promotion, as did opponents Southampton. The game ended goalless and both teams went up.

Spurs were back in the first division but needed more quality players to add to the up-and-coming Hoddle. Given Tottenham's history in the transfer market, a big signing or two was inevitable. But no-one expected two World Cup-winners to arrive.

Ricky Villa and Ossie Ardiles had just captured the football world's imagination as part of the

The transfer scoop of all time: Keith Burkinshaw (centre) captures Argentinian World Cup-winners Ricky Villa (left) and Ossie Ardiles in 1978

Glenn Hoddle

For most of his playing career, Glenn Hoddle was either loved or loathed. To Spurs supporters he was a godlike figure, the most talented English player of his generation. But his critics mistrusted his superb skills in an era when "work-rate" was the buzzword. Foreign stars such as Ossie Ardiles and Michel Platini could not believe that the England side was not built around Hoddle, as successive managers played him and dropped him at will. The fact that he won only 53 caps in a period when English football was short of truly world-class players is shameful.

Hoddle found fame abroad with Monaco, after leaving Spurs in 1987 having scored 110 goals in 491 games. He returned as player-manager of Swindon and then Chelsea and is now leading England out of the Dark Ages as national manager.

Argentina side that had won the World Cup as hosts in the summer of 1978.

Their joint transfer to Tottenham was front-page news and caused unprecedented interest. It started well, with Villa scoring in a 1–1 draw at Nottingham Forest. But the pair's home debut ended in a 4–1 defeat by Aston Villa and three games later Spurs were hammered 7–0 at Liverpool, the biggest losing margin in their League history.

Burkinshaw had to curb the attacking instincts of Ardiles, Villa and Hoddle, but lacking a prolific goalscorer Spurs finished in mid-table for the next two seasons.

Burkinshaw moved quickly to sign Steve Archibald from Aberdeen and Garth Crooks from Stoke and the pair hit it off instantly, leading Spurs to another FA Cup win in one of the most memorable finals of all time. No-one can tire of seeing Ricky Villa weaving his magic to mesmerize the Manchester City defence before scoring a fantastic goal in the final minutes of the reply at Wembley. "Ossie's Dream" of winning the cup for "Tottingham" had been achieved in wonderful style and more Wembley success was to follow (see Chapter Four – Up for the Cup).

But the 1982 win over QPR, again after a replay, was achieved without Ardiles and Villa, who had diplomatically been left out while the Falklands con-flict between Britain and Argentina raged. Ardiles moved to Paris St-Germain in France for a year on loan and broke his leg soon after returning, while Villa was never the same and left for America in 1983.

The centenary year, 1982, was also the year of Tottenham's first Wembley final defeat, losing 2–1 to Liverpool in extra time in the Milk Cup final. In Europe, Spurs were literally kicked out of the Cup-winners' Cup by Barcelona's brutal tactics in the semi-final.

The following season's European campaign ended in Munich, but 1984 brought the memories of those glory, glory nights of the Sixties back to White Hart Lane, with stand-in keeper Tony Parks becoming the hero in a dramatic penalty shoot-out win over Anderlecht of Belgium. By then, Burkinshaw had decided to quit after a growing feeling of disenchantment with the new board, led by property developer Irving Scholar.

The board had decided to float the club on the Stock Exchange and Burkinshaw felt that Tottenham Hotspur plc was being run more as a business than a football club. As he remarked famously when he left: "There used to be a football club there." But he left with his head high, having brought style and glamour back to White Hart Lane.

Fans' delight: Glenn Hoddle takes to the skies

1984 and all that

Burkinshaw's successor was his former assistant Peter Shreeves, as the board decided to appoint from within. With the addition of Chris Waddle and Paul Allen, Shreeves took Spurs to within touching distance of another championship before losing out to Everton. The following season he added Clive Allen, cousin of Paul and son of double-winner Les, but Spurs ended a disappointing 10th.

Shreeves was in turn replaced in the summer of 1986 by former Luton manager David Pleat, who believed in imaginative, attacking football. He signed Dundee United defender Richard Gough and made him captain, Steve Perryman having left for Oxford after a club record 854 appearances. Pleat also changed tactics early in the season, playing Clive Allen on his own in front of a five-man midfield that included Ardiles, Hoddle and Waddle.

It worked with spectacular success as Spurs became the great entertainers once again. Clive Allen scored a

One of Spurs' greatest players, Paul Gascoigne cost the club £2 million – then a club record – when he joined from Newcastle in 1988

record 49 goals that season and won Footballer of the Year and Player of the Year, but could not cap it with an FA Cup-winners' medal. Having lost to Arsenal in the semi-final of the League Cup, Spurs then lost their first-ever FA Cup final when Coventry came from behind to win 3–2, with Gary Mabbutt scoring an own goal after putting Spurs ahead.

Hoddle, having had a disappointing end to his Spurs career, left for Monaco, Ray Clemence suffered an injury that effectively ended his career and Ardiles was sold to QPR, Roberts to Chelsea and Gough to Glasgow Rangers. Half the team had gone.

But the bombshell came in October 1987 when Pleat was questioned by police for an alleged kerb-crawling incident. It was hugely embarrassing for the club and Pleat resigned, to be replaced by Terry Venables who had been sacked by Barcelona a few weeks earlier.

Venables had a major rebuilding job on his hands which he grasped with mixed success. His first major move was to sign Paul Gascoigne from Newcastle for a British record £2 million. He also brought in striker Paul Stewart from Manchester City for £1.7 million. Both took time to settle in, with Gascoigne becoming an instant crowd favourite but Stewart suffering the opposite fate. Waddle took over as Tottenham's saviour on the field, having his best-ever season for the club.

Venables brought back Gary Lineker from Barcelona in July 1989 to link up with Waddle and Gascoigne, but days later Waddle was sold to Marseilles for a staggering £4.25 million, a record fee for a British player. The club said it was too good to turn down, but supporters were shocked – as was Lineker.

The following season was moderately successful, with Spurs finishing third and Lineker and Gascoigne playing starring roles in the 1990 World Cup.

But there were serious financial problems. The board had over-reached themselves and Spurs were deeply in debt. Amid rumours that chairman and major shareholder Scholar was planning to sell out to publishing tycoon Robert Maxwell, Venables began to put together a consortium to buy the club. He eventually approached Amstrad Chairman Alan Sugar who then took the lead in negotiating the terms of the buy-out and together then bought out Scholar to save Spurs from going into liquidation.

Meanwhile, on the field, Gascoigne was inspiring Spurs on an amazing FA Cup run. The enigmatic midfielder was struggling with injury but he kept Spurs on course for the final and scored one of the greatest

Paul Gascoigne

Outrageous, enigmatic, brilliant, mad, tearful – there were no half-measures when Paul Gascoigne was playing for Spurs. He may have calmed down a little now, but the brilliant Geordie's career at Tottenham was a roller-coaster ride of highs and lows.

Signed from Newcastle for a record £2 million in 1988, he took a while to settle in but then showed why he was considered the best British player for years. "Gazza" became a household name during the 1990 World Cup, and then returned to inspire Spurs to FA Cup victory, securing a place in every supporter's heart with that free kick against Arsenal in the semi-final. His subsequent injury in the final almost killed off his move to Lazio, but he spent three years in Italy before making a sensational move to Glasgow Rangers in 1995.

goals ever seen at Wembley, with a ferocious free-kick against the old enemies, Arsenal, in the semi-final.

That 3–1 win, the first semi-final played at Wembley, ended Arsenal's hopes of doing another Double and meant Spurs were back at Wembley to face Nottingham Forest. By now money was needed to keep the club going and a tentative deal was struck with Lazio to take Gascoigne to Italy for £8.5 million.

But when he suffered a serious knee injury in the opening minutes of the final, it looked like the deal would be scrapped. Spurs won without Gazza (see Chapter Four – Up for the Cup) and lifted the FA Cup for a record eighth time.

The Lazio deal was resurrected but at a reduced fee of £5.5 million after Gascoigne spent the next season recuperating. Venables, now on the board, became chief executive and brought back Peter Shreeves as manager.

League form was indifferent and Spurs went out of the Cup-winners' Cup to Feyenoord in the quarter-finals. As the season drew to a close, Lineker announced that he would be going to the new J-League in Japan to end his career, meaning that Spurs were about to enter the brave new dawn of the Premiership without a major crowd-pleasing star.

Gary Mabbutt proudly displays the FA Cup in 1991. Spurs won the Cup for the eighth time, unfortunately without Paul Gascoigne, who badly injured his knee in the final

Spurs Premiership History

As one of Britain's biggest clubs, Spurs have rarely been out of the headlines – and the Premiership years have been no different

TOTTENHAM'S history in the first five years of the FA Premiership has been typical of the club's fortunes except for one important aspect - they have not won anything. Throughout the preceding years the Spurs story has been one of ups and downs, big-name signings, off-the-field wrangles with authority and a team that can enchant and frustrate in equal measure.

The Premiership years have been no different. Big names have come and gone, the club has made headlines for all sorts of reasons and the side has threatened more than once to win major honours. That it has not yet happened is a major source of frustration for everyone at the club – players, staff and supporters.

Spurs have finished no higher than seventh in that time, despite having more than a passing acquaintance with serious championship challenges over the years. But they have also flirted with relegation, had points deducted and then restored, been banned from Europe and reinstated and come close to Cup glory. Clearly a club like Tottenham should be winning things: tradition suggests it, players want it and fans demand it.

But unhappy supporters would do well to remem-

David Ginola's £2 million signing from Newcastle brought yet another flamboyant star to Spurs

ber that the long history of the club, glittering as it may be, has been punctuated with long barren periods when nothing was won at all.

The FA Cup wins of 1901 and 1921 were followed by inexplicable slumps when Spurs were expected to go on to greater things. The club even spent 15 years outside the top flight either side of the Second World War. Even Arthur Rowe's great Championship-winning side of the early 1950s failed to follow up their great promise. Bill Nicholson has been the only Spurs manager to deliver success consistently, and many have been frustrated since.

Football has undoubtedly changed since the first-division clubs broke away from the Football League to form the Premier League in 1992. The huge amounts of money brought in by television and merchandising have raised the stakes for all concerned, and the net result is that the glittering prizes are spread among fewer clubs than before.

But Tottenham are still one of the biggest clubs in Britain and famous throughout the world. They can still attract world-class players to White Hart Lane and the fans turn up in their thousands.

Having survived bankruptcy by the skin of their teeth in the year before the Premier League was formed, Spurs were at a financial disadvantage when the big spenders went into overdrive and transfer fees began to spiral. But a combination of prudent administration, excellent commercial acumen and time devoted to the club's famous youth policy means that Tottenham are still able to look forward to the future with confidence.

Steffen Iversen's first goal for Spurs against Southampton. He chose Spurs over top European clubs

Season 1992–93

15 AUG: Andy Turner becomes the Premiership's youngest player when he makes his debut for Spurs in a goalless draw at Southampton aged 17 years, 145 days. Darren Anderton also makes his Spurs debut.

19 AUG: Spurs crash 2–0 at home to Coventry and Gordon Durie is booked by referee Dermot Gallagher for allegedly feigning injury in an attempt to get an opponent sent off.

28 AUG: Former Millwall striker Teddy Sheringham joins from Nottingham Forest for £2.1 million. He scores on his home debut against Sheffield United a week later in a 2–0 victory.

30 AUG: A Jason Cundy wonder-goal from the half-way line helps Spurs to a 1–1 draw at Ipswich, and takes them off the bottom of the table for the first time this season.

5 SEPT: Andy Turner becomes the youngest scorer in the Premiership when he scores a last-minute winner in the 2–1 win over Everton at the age of 17 years, 166 days.

23 SEPT: Former Tottenham favourite Paul Gascoigne scores for Lazio against Spurs in a friendly in Rome, his first senior game since the 1991 FA Cup Final. The game finishes 3–0 to the Italians and Gazza looks sharp and fit.

31 OCT: Nayim scores one of the goals of the season against Liverpool at White Hart lane in the League when he volleys in a 40-yard effort in a 2–0 win. Neil Ruddock adds the second and Tottenham finally look to have their season on track.

1 DEC: Spurs' interest in the Coca-Cola Cup comes to an end at the hands of Nottingham Forest, who go through to the fifth round with goals from Ian Woan and Roy Keane.

5 DEC: Sol Campbell makes his debut as a goal-scoring substitute in the 2–1 home defeat by London rivals Chelsea, for whom Eddie Newton scores twice.

5 JAN: Non-League Marlow are thrashed 5–1 at White Hart Lane in the third round of the FA Cup. Originally

Darren Anderton took a while to settle after his move from Portsmouth but was soon a favourite

drawn at home, they choose to give up their home advantage in favour of a good pay-day in front of a big crowd.

19 JAN: Spurs reach the FA Cup fifth round with a 2–0 win over League leaders Norwich at Carrow Road. Teddy Sheringham scores both goals as his understanding with teenager Nick Barmby continues to flourish.

13 FEB: FA Cup progress continues with a 3–2 win against Wimbledon. Sheringham, Barmby and Anderton score to put Spurs 3–0 up by half-time.

20 FEB: Sheringham scores a hat-trick in the 4–0 defeat of Leeds to avenge their 5–0 win at Elland Road earlier in the season, in which Eric Cantona scored a hat-trick.

27 FEB: Sheringham and Anderton score in a 3–2 win over QPR, Spurs' sixth victory in succession. But it is the last game for Barmby before he leaves for the World Youth Cup in Australia.

2 MAR: The impressive run earns Doug Livermore the Manager of the Month award but it all ends in a 6–0 thrashing at Sheffield United, with substitute John Hendry breaking two fingers.

6 MAR: Spurs march into the semi-finals of the FA Cup after an impressive 4–2 win over Manchester City at Maine Road. Home fans invade the pitch 10 minutes before the end of the game, but police restore order.

6 APR: The FA Cup run is ended at Wembley as Spurs lose the semi-final to eventual winners Arsenal, revenge for their 1991 defeat. Tony Adams scores the game's only goal 11 minutes from time.

12 APR: Goalkeeper Erik Thorstvedt breaks a bone in his hand as Spurs go down 2–1 at doomed Nottingham Forest. It is also the last game for Nayim, who is returning to his native Spain with Real Zaragoza.

8 MAY: Another heavy defeat at Anfield as a side containing youngsters David McDonald, Lee Hodges, Danny Hill and Kevin Watson loses 6–2 to Liverpool.

11 MAY: Spurs beat Arsenal 3–1 at Highbury in the final League game of the season, with two goals from Hendry and one by Teddy Sheringham, who secures the Golden Boot as the Premiership's top scorer.

14 MAY: Sensational news as Chairman Alan Sugar calls an emergency board meeting and Terry Venables is sacked as chief executive. He is reinstated by the High Court for a further 10 days but eventually leaves a month later.

Teddy Sheringham ended his first Spurs season as the Premiership's top scorer with 22 League goals

Season 1993–94

19 JUN: Former Argentinian superstar Ossie Ardiles is appointed manager with Doug Livermore becoming coach. West Bromwich Albion complain about Tottenham's approach for Ardiles, who was in charge at the Hawthorns.

6 JULY: Ray Clemence is sacked as first–team coach, and former Spurs captain Steve Perryman joins from Watford to become assistant manager to Ardiles.

21 JULY: Defender Neil Ruddock has his transfer request approved and he leaves for Graeme Souness's Liverpool in a £2.5 million deal after just one year back at Spurs.

31 JULY: Paul Gascoigne returns to White Hart Lane for the Makita International tournament. Tottenham beat Lazio 3–2 before losing 4–0 to Chelsea in the final a day later.

3 AUG: Midfielder Jason Dozzell is signed from Ipswich for a tribunal-set fee of £1.75 million. A week later, defender Colin Calderwood signs from Swindon Town for another tribunal-set fee of £1.25 million.

14 AUG: On the opening day of the season Ossie Ardiles returns to Newcastle, the club that sacked him as manager 18 months earlier, and gains revenge with Spurs winning 1–0 thanks to a Teddy Sheringham goal.

25 AUG: A famous night at Anfield as two goals from Sheringham give Tottenham only their third League win at Liverpool in 82 years. It is also their third League win in four games.

One of many tense moments for manager Ossie Ardiles (left) and his assistant Steve Perryman

2 SEPT: Terry Venables is ousted from the Spurs board after selling the majority of his 23.3 per cent shareholding for around £3 million. Spurs also settle out of court with West Brom over the Ardiles affair.

18 SEPT: A remarkable 5–0 defeat of Oldham, with Spurs scoring three goals inside three minutes at the start of the game, puts them fifth in the table, but right-back Dean Austin breaks his leg.

6 OCT: Spurs beat Burnley in the Coca-Cola Cup, winning 3–1 at home after a goalless first leg, but Darren Caskey is sent off and striker Gordon Durie openly swears at Ardiles as he is substituted.

15 OCT: Durie is put on the transfer list after his bust-up with Ardiles and eventually moves back to Scotland with Glasgow Rangers for £1.2 million a month later.

16 OCT: Sheringham is injured in a 2–1 defeat at Manchester United. A foul by Bryan Robson puts the striker out of action until the following April.

17 OCT: Mixed fortunes: the club is charged with misconduct for poaching Ardiles from West Brom but announces a profit of £3.3 million the next day.

27 OCT: A 1–0 win over Derby County at the Baseball Ground sees Spurs into the fourth round of the Coca-Cola Cup. Nick Barmby is the scorer, having recovered from an operation for shin splints earlier in the season.

5 NOV: Arthur Rowe, the manager of the 1951 League-winning side, dies at the age of 85. By a strange coincidence his greatest signing, Danny Blanchflower, is to die only a month later.

24 NOV: Gary Mabbutt sustains a severe facial injury in a clash with John Fashanu of Wimbledon. Mabbutt is taken off the pitch unconscious on a stretcher and rushed to hospital for emergency surgery to a smashed eye-socket.

1 DEC: A young Sol Campbell is played as a makeshift striker against Blackburn Rovers in the Coca-Cola Cup. He scores the only goal as Spurs beat Kenny Dalglish's side at White Hart Lane.

6 DEC: Campbell plays up-front again as the north London derby finishes 1–1 at Highbury. A fantastic

Gary Mabbutt survived shocking facial injuries after a clash with Wimbledon's John Fashanu

1 JAN: A 2–1 defeat at home to Coventry City is the beginning of a seven-game losing streak in the League that sees Spurs slip to the fringe of the relegation zone.

12 JAN: Spurs go out of one Cup when they lose 2–1 to Aston Villa in the quarter-final of the Coca-Cola Cup at White Hart Lane.

26 JAN: "Rocket" Ronny Rosenthal, as he comes to be known by fans, is signed from Liverpool for £250,000. The Israeli international striker scores on his debut the following week but it cannot stop a 3–1 defeat by Sheffield Wednesday.

10 FEB: 80 days and several operations after the Fashanu incident, captain Gary Mabbutt makes his comeback in a reserve game against Chelsea wearing a face-mask to protect his shattered cheek.

2 MAR: Rosenthal scores again in a 1–1 draw against Aston Villa that ends a run of seven consecutive defeats, but Villa's Mark Bosnich saves two penalties.

9 MAR: Darren Anderton makes a promising debut for England in the 1–0 win over Denmark in Terry Venables's first game as national coach.

2 APR: Teddy Sheringham marks his return after five months out with a goal against Norwich in a 2–1 win that eases fears of relegation.

first-half goal from Darren Anderton is equalled by Ian Wright in the second half.

9 DEC: Danny Blanchflower, the captain of the 1961 Double-winning side, and one of the true greats of British football, dies after a long illness at the age of 67.

23 APR: Tottenham defeat fellow-strugglers Southampton 3–0 at White Hart Lane to take the pressure off manager Ossie Ardiles.

2 MAY: A 2–0 win at Oldham with goals from Vinny Samways and David Howells gives Spurs the win they need, finally ending all thoughts of relegation: they eventually end the season in 15th place.

Season 1994–95

12 JUNE: Tottenham are fined £600,000, banned from the FA Cup for one season and have 12 points deducted before the season starts as punishment for financial irregularities under a previous administration.

2 JULY: Chairman Alan Sugar vows to fight the punishment and wins back six points on appeal, but the fine is increased from £600,000 to £1.5 million and the FA Cup ban still stands.

4 JULY: Midfielder Steve Sedgley leaves Tottenham for Ipswich in a £1 million deal and Vinny Samways joins Everton soon afterwards for £2.2 million.

28 JULY: Ossie Ardiles announces the signing of Romanian World Cup star Ilie Dumitrescu from Steaua Bucharest for £2.6 million. The attacking midfielder had been a star of the 1994 USA World Cup finals.

30 JULY: Spurs stun the football world by signing German superstar Jürgen Klinsmann from Monaco for £2 million. Klinsmann's arrival immediately boosts Tottenham's stock market valuation and shortens their title odds.

20 AUGUST: Klinsmann makes a storming start to his English career by scoring against Sheffield Wednesday in the opening day's 4–3 win.

24 AUG: Klinsmann has a sensational home debut, thrilling the White Hart Lane crowd by scoring with an overhead kick and a header as Spurs beat Everton 2–1.

12 SEPT: Defensive lapses cost Spurs dearly as they lose 2–1 to Southampton, who score two late goals. It is the first of three successive League defeats.

16 SEPT: Romanian midfielder Gica Popescu is signed from PSV Eindhoven for £2.9 million to complete a trio of foreign stars snapped up following the USA World Cup finals.

21 SEPT: Klinsmann hits a hat-trick as Spurs win 6–3 at Watford in the League Cup, but Spurs only scrape through after losing the second leg 3–2 at home two weeks later.

Jürgen Klinsmann scores on his debut, at Sheffield Wednesday, before being carried off with an injury

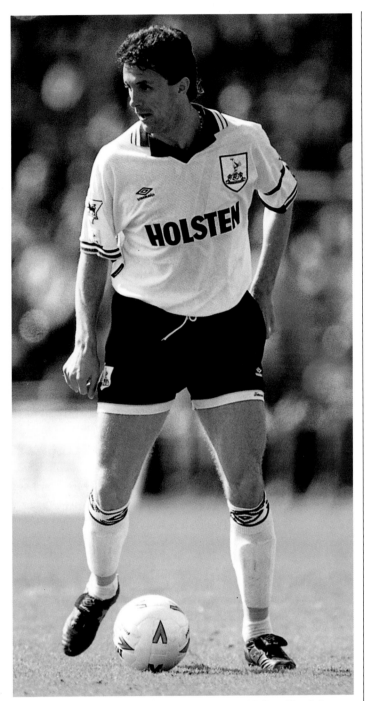

Gica Popescu never settled in at White Hart Lane and left for Barcelona after only one season

4 OCT: Darren Anderton signs a new long-term contract but then tears a thigh muscle that keeps him out of action for six weeks.

26 OCT: Pressure mounts on Ossie Ardiles when Spurs lose 3–0 to the first division's bottom club, Notts County, in the League Cup. Dumitrescu is sent off.

29 OCT: Tottenham beat West Ham 3–1 for their

first home win since August but it is not enough to save Ardiles, who is sacked two days later. His assistant Steve Perryman takes over as caretaker manager for one match.

15 NOV: Gerry Francis, having left QPR during a power struggle, takes charge of Spurs on a one-year rolling contract. Two days later the team's defensive problems are highlighted as they lose 3–4 at home to Aston Villa in his first game.

9 DEC: Celebrations as an arbitration tribunal overturns the FA's punishment, reinstating Tottenham in the FA Cup and overturning the six-point deduction, although the £1.5 million fine still stands.

30 DEC: Out-of-favour Romanian midfielder Ilie Dumitrescu is sent on loan to Seville in Spain until the end of the season.

7 JAN: Spurs beat Altrincham 3–0 in the FA Cup third round, their 10th game unbeaten, and equal a club record run of six successive clean sheets.

5 FEB: Eventual champions Blackburn Rovers are ripped apart 3–1 by a rampant Tottenham attack at White Hart Lane in the League. Klinsmann, Anderton and Barmby grab the goals.

1 MAR: A Ronny Rosenthal hat-trick helps see off Southampton 6–2 in an extraordinary FA Cup replay at The Dell, with Spurs coming back from 2–0 down at half-time to win in extra time.

11 MAR: The highlight of Tottenham's season comes as they beat Liverpool 2–1 in their FA Cup quarter-final at Anfield, with Klinsmann scoring a dramatic last-minute winner.

9 APR: The FA Cup dream dies at Elland Road as Joe Royle's Everton hammer an injury-hit Spurs 4–1. A Klinsmann penalty is scant consolation as the Merseysiders run rampant.

11 MAY: Jürgen Klinsmann ends weeks of speculation that he will leave Spurs by confirming that he is to return to Germany with Bayern Munich.

22 MAY: Gica Popescu signs for Barcelona for £3.1 million after an unsettled eight months in England.

Season 1995–96

13 JUNE: Tottenham sign a record four-year kit deal worth more than £10 million with manufacturers Pony.

21 JUNE: Chris Armstrong is signed from Crystal Palace for a club record £4.5 million as a replacement for German striker Jürgen Klinsmann.

25 JUNE: Tottenham reluctantly enter the InterToto Cup to save English clubs being banned from Europe. They field a team of youngsters and play home games at Brighton's Goldstone Ground, incurring a one-year ban from Europe by UEFA.

4 JULY: Pre-season injuries to Teddy Sheringham, Darren Anderton and free transfer signing Clive Wilson throw Gerry Francis's plans into turmoil. Anderton undergoes a hernia operation which keeps him out for the first month of the season.

Record signing Chris Armstrong quickly built up a productive partnership with Teddy Sheringham

5 AUG: Nick Barmby leaves to join Bryan Robson's Middlesbrough for £5.25 million. The young England star, having recently signed a new long-term deal, claims he is homesick for the North.

19 AUG: Teddy Sheringham scores in a 1–1 draw at Manchester City on the opening day of the season.

30 AUG: A draw at West Ham means that Spurs are rooted to the foot of the table, having failed to manage a win in their first four games of the campaign.

9 SEPT: A 2–1 home victory over Leeds with goals from Sheringham and David Howells is the start of a four-game winning streak that sees Tottenham slowly climb up the table.

25 SEPT: The luckless Anderton tears a groin muscle during a 3–2 win at QPR, an injury that will force him to miss the next seven months of the season.

6 OCT: Ruel Fox is signed from Newcastle for £4.2 million. The former Norwich and England "B" winger is immediately impressive as Anderton's replacement.

22 OCT: Chris Armstrong scores his first League goal for the club as they get a 1–1 draw at Everton. It is to be the start of a purple patch for the striker.

25 OCT: Spurs are knocked out of the Coca-Cola Cup by Coventry City, who recover from a 2–0 half-time deficit to win 3–2.

18 NOV: Sheringham and Armstrong show their growing understanding with a goal apiece to beat Arsenal 2–1 at White Hart Lane.

16 DEC: A 1–0 win over Wimbledon thanks to a Ruel Fox goal puts Spurs third in the League and among the serious title-challengers.

1 JAN: In the performance of the season, Spurs hammer eventual champions Manchester United 4–1 at White Hart Lane. Chris Armstrong scores two while Teddy Sheringham and Sol Campbell grab one apiece in a sensational win.

12 JAN: UEFA ban Spurs and Wimbledon from European competition for a year for fielding weakened sides in the previous summer's InterToto Cup.

World Cup star Ilie Dumitrescu cost Spurs £2.6 million but left to join West Ham in March 1996

18 JAN: Andy Sinton is signed from Sheffield Wednesday for £1.5 million to be reunited with Gerry Francis, his former manager at QPR. The club announce record pre-tax profits of more than £7 million for the previous half-year.

26 JAN: Alan Sugar has UEFA's one-year European ban lifted after he proves that Claude Littner had obtained the written permission of the FA and UEFA to field the side they did and to play at an away ground.

7 FEB: Wolves are beaten 2–0 in an FA Cup fourth-round replay at Molineux after a 1–1 draw at White Hart Lane. Ronny Rosenthal and Teddy Sheringham are the two scorers in an excellent team performance.

19 FEB: The televised fifth round FA Cup game at Nottingham Forest is called off after 15 minutes because of a snowstorm. Spurs draw 2–2 when the game is replayed a week later.

2 MAR: The Romanian connection finally comes to an end as Ilie Dumitrescu joins West Ham for £1.5 million following work permit problems.

9 MAR: Spurs go out of the FA Cup 3–1 on penalties at home to Nottingham Forest after a 1–1 draw. Forest keeper Mark Crossley is in inspired form as his side advance.

27 MAR: Darren Anderton plays his first competitive game since September – a 45-minute outing in a reserve game. He comes through unscathed.

27 APR: A 1–1 draw against Chelsea at home sees Tottenham complete April without a win in the League, leaving qualification for Europe in doubt.

2 MAY: Anderton scores twice in a superb 3–1 win at Leeds to prove his fitness for Euro '96 and put Spurs back in with a chance of qualifying for Europe.

5 MAY: Jason Dozzell gives Spurs the lead against Newcastle on the final day of the season, but the Magpies equalise and, to make matters worse, the final UEFA Cup spot goes to Arsenal.

Season 1996–97

21 JULY: Danish footballer of the year Allan Nielsen is signed from Brondby for £1.6 million, but he cannot join the squad until after the Danish side's Champions' League qualifier on 22 August.

17 AUG: The season starts off on a disappointing note when, despite a superb 2–0 win at Blackburn, inspirational captain Gary Mabbutt breaks his leg after 18 minutes – an injury that will keep him out for the rest of the season.

24 AUG: A 0–0 draw at home against high-flying Everton comes at a price: Chris Armstrong turns his ankle – an injury that will eventually need an operation and keep him out for most of the season – and strike partner Teddy Sheringham is also injured.

4 SEPT: Vinnie Jones is sent off for a violent challenge on Darren Anderton in a controversial defeat at Wimbledon. Jones claims Anderton spat at him but

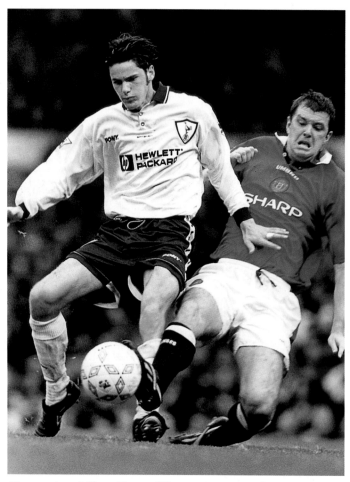

Teenage striker Rory Allen was one of the few bright spots in a disappointing 1996–97 season

the Spurs player denies it, saying: "You'd have to be mad to spit at Vinnie Jones".

7 SEPT: Teenage striker Rory Allen scores against Newcastle on his full debut, in place of the injured Sheringham, but Kevin Keegan's men run out 2–1 winners.

25 SEPT: Gerry Francis announces that Anderton will need yet another hernia operation. Once again injuries will play a large part in keeping the England midfielder out of action for long periods of the season.

12 OCT: Controversy as Aston Villa goalkeeper Mark Bosnich makes a Nazi salute at Spurs fans during Tottenham's 1–0 win, the first in the Premiership at home this season. Bosnich later apologises to fans and shakes hands with chairman Alan Sugar.

23 OCT: Progress is made in the Coca-Cola Cup against Sunderland as Peter Reid's men are beaten 2–1 at White Hart Lane with a last-minute goal by Sol Campbell.

26 OCT: Spurs offer to call off their game against Chelsea after the death of the Blues' vice-chairman Matthew Harding in a helicopter crash, but the game goes on and Ruud Gullit's men win 3–1 in a funereal atmosphere at Stamford Bridge.

22 NOV: Spurs successfully beat off some of Europe's leading clubs to sign Norwegian Under-21 striker Steffen Iversen from Rosenborg for £2.6 million, although he will not be able to join for another two weeks.

24 NOV: A bad month begins with a 3–1 defeat at Arsenal, with the Gunners grabbing two goals in the last five minutes against the run of play. It brings to an end a run of five wins in six games.

27 NOV: Things get worse as Bolton hammer Spurs 6–1 in the fourth round of the Coca-Cola Cup. The first-division side, with a history of giant-killing, had already knocked out Chelsea's expensive foreign legion.

2 DEC: The bad luck continues as Liverpool win 2–0 at White Hart Lane with a freak goal from Steve MacManaman. Ian Walker has his shot covered until the ball hits a divot and flies over the stranded keeper.

5 DEC: John Scales is signed from Liverpool for £2.6 million after turning down a move to Leeds. The England international central defender once played alongside Gerry Francis at Bristol Rovers.

12 DEC: Chris Armstrong finally has an ankle operation that is expected to keep him out for six weeks. But the wound fails to heal properly and the striker does not play again all season.

28 DEC: Another low point, as Spurs crash 7–1 at Newcastle, their worst defeat in the Premiership and their heaviest loss for 16 years. Ironically, Newcastle's manager Kevin Keegan decides to resign after the game.

5 JAN: An injury-hit team, including teenage strikers Rory Allen and Neale Fenn, perform admirably at Old Trafford but go down 2–0 to rampant Manchester United in the third round of the FA Cup.

8 JAN: Swiss defender Ramon Vega joins for £3.5 million, six months after turning down Spurs to move to Cagliari in Italy. He makes his debut against Manchester United the following week but Spurs go down 2–1.

4 MAR: After a depressing run of seven defeats in nine games, Spurs finally turn on the style to win 4–0 at Sunderland, with Steffen Iversen hitting a stunning hat-trick.

11 MAY: Coventry win 2–1 at White Hart Lane after a delayed kick-off on a tense last day of the season to ensure their Premiership survival and leave Spurs in 10th position.

13 MAY: Sol Campbell signs a new contract that will keep him at White Hart Lane for another four years. The central defender has become a fixture in the England side.

16 MAY: Sheringham asks for a transfer after failing to agree terms on a new contract. Spurs decide to let him go.

27 JUNE: Sheringham is transferred to up north to League Champions Manchester United for a fee of £3.5 million and Spurs are immediately linked with a deal to sign Les Ferdinand from Newcastle as his replacement.

27 JULY: Spurs sign Ferdinand for a new club record £6 million to complete a double swoop from Newcastle, having taken French winger David Ginola for £2 million two weeks earlier.

Gerry Francis spent nearly £10 million on players in summer 1997, including winger José Dominguez

Chapter 3

Spurs in Europe

Spurs have a great history in Europe, and Liverpool are the only British team with more European trophies. Here we recall some of Tottenham's glory, glory nights.

European Overview

Many of today's younger football fans may well believe Manchester United were the first successful English club in Europe, when they beat Benfica to win the European Cup in 1968. Even Liverpool's four European Cup wins and Nottingham Forest's two victories failed to receive the glowing accolades that were heaped upon the late Sir Matt Busby and his classic Sixties side.

But in fact Spurs had beaten them to it five years earlier, becoming the first British side to win a European trophy and put English football on the Continental map.

Long before United were to triumph at Wembley, Bill Nicholson's double-winning Spurs side had shown that they could not only conquer the best England could muster but also put one over on the best from the Continent, by winning the European Cup-winners' Cup. And this was only a year after coming so close to winning the European Cup, when Benfica beat them in a controversial semi-final in 1962.

That was the beginning of the glory, glory nights at White Hart Lane, the first British ground to become a really intimidating cauldron for foreign teams.

When Polish champions Gornik Zabrze arrived with a 4–2 lead in September 1961 they were greeted with a barrage of noise from over 60,000 unashamedly partisan home fans that even the Spurs players found spine-tingling. With such support, it was no wonder Spurs won 8–1 at the start of a very special relationship between White Hart Lane and European football.

If that cup run announced to Europe that England finally had a team capable of taking on and beating their best, then the following year Spurs proved it. Their breathtaking 5–1 Cup-winners' Cup Final victory over Atletico Madrid in Rotterdam was the crowning achievement of Nicholson's double-winning side, and put Spurs on the world map. Sadly, they were not to achieve the same giddy heights during the Sixties, despite an FA Cup Final win in 1967.

Nicholson had to wait until the early 1970s to see European success again, when the 1972 UEFA Cup triumph over Wolves made Spurs the first English club to win two European trophies.

It was a record they eventually surrendered to Liverpool, who beat them in the semi-final of the same competition the following year.

A year later Spurs again reached the UEFA Cup final, but lost to Feyenoord in a game that placed a black mark against Tottenham's European record when rioting fans stole the headlines. The shame of English football was felt especially by Bill Nicholson, and it must have added to his view that football was changing in a way that he found went against all his beliefs, both on and off the pitch. He was to resign a few months later.

It was left to Keith Burkinshaw to lead Spurs out of the doldrums and back into Europe. With the masterful Glenn Hoddle prompting from midfield, Burkinshaw's Spurs saw a golden era at the start of the 1980s, winning two FA Cups and the UEFA Cup again. That thrilling win on penalties over Anderlecht on a memorable night in 1984 was also Burkinshaw's swansong as he too left White Hart Lane, a disenchanted man, a short while later.

The victory was to be Tottenham's last success in Europe before the five-year ban on English clubs following the Heysel Stadium disaster.

The five-year ban left English sides playing catch-up with the rest of Europe when they returned at the start of the 1990s. Tottenham's sole venture after the 1991 FA Cup success ended in a quarter-final defeat, again at the hands of their European arch-rivals Feyenoord.

Three times under Gerry Francis Spurs have had strong hopes of qualifying for Europe only to see them dashed at the end of the season. With the money and prestige European competition brings, as well as the development of players, it is vital that Tottenham get back into Europe as soon as possible.

The fans deserve it, too. Ever since the night in 1961 when Gornik were terrified into submission by the electric atmosphere created by more than 60,000 raucous fans, White Hart Lane has had a special relationship with Europe. It would be wonderful to see those glory, glory nights back at the Lane.

1961 European Cup semi-final, second leg: Bobby Smith gets Spurs's first in the 2–1 defeat of Benfica

The Sixties

European Cup 1961–62

Tottenham's double-winning triumph gave Bill Nicholson's all-conquering side the chance to wipe the floor with Europe in the same imperious manner as they had dealt with domestic opposition.

But it didn't start as well as everyone had thought it would. A 4–2 defeat in Poland by the miners of Gornik Zabrze saw the English champions booed off the park.

But in the return at White Hart Lane, any fears of an early European Cup exit were soon forgotten as Spurs swept Gornik aside with an astonishing 8–1 victory to go through 10–5 on aggregate. Cliff Jones scored a 17-minute hat-trick in the first half as the Poles froze in front of a huge and noisy crowd.

The second round paired Nicholson's side with Dutch masters Feyenoord – the first meeting between

Spurs' 5–1 demolition of Atletico Madrid in Rotterdam won them the 1963 European Cup-winners' Cup

two teams whose paths in Europe were to cross many more times. A 3–1 win in the first leg in Holland gave Spurs the upper hand, despite Nicholson's claim that his side had merely "muddled through". Another huge crowd of 62,144 packed into White Hart Lane for the second leg and they were rocked by an early Feyenoord goal, but Terry Dyson equalized four minutes later.

The draw was enough to earn them a trip to Dukla Prague in the third round, and a tactical defensive game meant Spurs came away trailing by a single goal. It was never going to be enough for the Czechoslovakians, and two goals apiece from Dave Mackay and Bobby Smith saw Spurs through to the semi-final with a 4–2 aggregate win.

Tottenham stood just two games away from a place in the European Cup Final at the first attempt. In front of a hostile Portuguese crowd of 70,000 Spurs tried hard to cope with a rampant Benfica.

Bobby Smith scored once and Jimmy Greaves had two "goals" ruled out on his European debut for Spurs, as Benfica won 3–1.

The return leg was a night to remember as Spurs threw everything at the Portuguese champions, in a game later described by one distinguished journalist as "the most electrifying 90 minutes of European football I have ever seen on an English ground".

Benfica scored against the run of play to take a 4–1 aggregate lead before Greaves had another effort controversially disallowed. But goals from Smith and Blanchflower either side of half-time left Spurs with one goal to score in the remaining 40 minutes.

Despite hitting the woodwork three times, they could not find a way through. Tottenham's European dream was over – for a year, at least.

European Cup-winners' Cup 1962–63

An FA Cup victory over Burnley earned Nicholson's side another trip to foreign fields and the chance to ease the agony of their previous season's European Cup exit.

A bye in the opening round was followed by some awe-inspiring football as Spurs won the "Battle of Britain" against Glasgow Rangers. An emphatic 5–2 success in the first leg at White Hart Lane was followed by a 3–2 victory at Ibrox, with Bobby Smith scoring twice on his comeback from injury.

When Tottenham slammed Slovan Bratislava 6–2 on aggregate in the next round, Europe was beginning to notice the Spurs tide. Even the dismissal of Jimmy Greaves, the first of his career, in the first leg victory over OFK Belgrade in the semi-final failed to stop Tottenham's surge to the final. A 3–1 scoreline gave them a 5–2 aggregate win and a place in the final against Atletico Madrid of Spain.

The climax to a wonderful European campaign ended in glorious triumph in Rotterdam as Terry Dyson tore the Spanish defence to pieces. The little left-winger set up Jimmy Greaves for the first goal and then made it 2–0 himself.

Madrid pulled a goal back but Dyson then slung in a cross that the Spanish 'keeper fumbled into his own net. Greaves added a fourth before Dyson hit a 25–yard screamer into the net following a 30–yard run. Even without the injured Dave Mackay, and with Blanchflower not fully fit, Spurs swept the Spaniards aside and Nicholson became the very first British manager to lift a European trophy.

> ### First WIN
>
> **European Cup-winners' Cup Final**
>
> **15 May 1963** Feyenoord Stadium, Rotterdam – Attendance: 40,000
>
> **Tottenham Hotspur 5**
> *(Greaves 2, Dyson 2, White)*
> **Atletico Madrid 1**
>
> **Team:** Brown, Baker, Henry, Blanchflower, Norman, Marchi, Jones, White, R Smith, Greaves, Dyson.

European Cup-winners' Cup 1963–64

Qualifying as holders, Spurs started with a 2–0 win over Manchester United in the home leg of the first round, with goals from Mackay and Dyson. But Mackay broke his leg in the return at Old Trafford and 10-man Spurs went down 4–1.

European Cup-winners' Cup 1967–68

By 1967, a new side had emerged from the ashes of Nicholson's double-winning heroes. Victory over Chelsea in the FA Cup Final put Spurs back in Europe, and they saw off Hadjuk Split again with a 6–3 aggregate victory.

But French side Olympique Lyonnais put them out in the second round after a violent first-leg defeat in France that saw Alan Mullery sent off for retaliation. Spurs won the return leg 4–3 but it was simply not enough.

The Seventies

Bill Nicholson's reign as manager took another step towards greatness when he guided the club to a second era of success in the early Seventies. After winning the League Cup for the first time in 1971, Spurs were back in Europe in the new UEFA Cup, which had replaced the old Inter-City Fairs Cup.

UEFA Cup 1972

Tottenham, fresh from their League Cup triumph over Aston Villa, entered the UEFA Cup with a bang when Alan Gilzean and Martin Chivers scored eight goals between them in a thumping 15–1 aggregate victory over Iceland's Keflavik.

In the second round it took a 20–yard strike by Martin Peters in the home leg to dispose of French side Nantes. Chivers was to prove the key man in the next round against Rapid Bucharest. He hit two in the 3–0 home demolition of the Romanians and, along with Jimmy Pearce, grabbed one in the second leg.

The quarter-finals paired Spurs with another Romanian side, UT Arad. Goals from Roger Morgan and Mike England gave them a 2–0 away win, while an Alan Gilzean strike in a 1–1 draw at home made sure of a place in the semi-finals against the mighty AC Milan.

In a game which saw the violent side of Milan, Spurs rode the storm to record a 2–1 home-leg victory, thanks largely to their self-discipline and two fine goals from rising star Steve Perryman. In the away leg

Alan Mullery's team-mates lift him shoulder-high after his winning goal in the 1972 UEFA Cup

---

Second SUCCESS	
1st leg **3 May 1972** Molineux Stadium, Wolverhampton – Attendance: 38,362	2nd leg **17 May 1972** White Hart Lane, Tottenham – Attendance: 54,303
Wolverhampton Wanderers 1 Tottenham Hotspur 2 (Chivers 2)	**Tottenham Hotspur 1 Wolverhampton Wanderers 1** (Mullery)
Team: Jennings, Kinnear, Knowles, Mullery, England, Beal, Gilzean, Perryman, Chivers, Peters, Coates (Pratt)	**Team:** Jennings, Kinnear, Knowles, Mullery, England, Beal, coates, Perryman, Chivers, Peters, Gilzean

Alan Mullery scored a spectacular long-range equalizer for a 1–1 draw to put Spurs through to an all-English final against Wolves.

If Chivers was the star of the 2–1 first-leg win at Molineux, scoring both goals, it was Mullery who became the hero at White Hart Lane. Having been sent on loan to second-division Fulham two weeks before the final he was recalled for the second leg, and responded with a diving header to gain a 1–1 draw and win the trophy. Not that he knew much about it – he was knocked out when the ball went in! It was a marvellous swansong for the former Spurs skipper, who moved permanently to Fulham a few weeks later.

UEFA Cup 1972–73

As holders of the trophy, Spurs were given another chance in the UEFA Cup and almost made it two on the trot. A 12–3 aggregate victory over Lyn Oslo in the first round, with Chivers scoring five goals, started them in style and they followed up with a 4–1 aggregate win over Olympiakos Piraeus.

A potential upset against Red Star Belgrade was overcome by goals from Alan Gilzean and Martin Chivers at White Hart Lane as Spurs went through 2–1 on aggregate, while Chivers scored a valuable away goal to see off Portuguese side Vitoria Setubal in the quarter-finals.

That victory set up a semi-final against Liverpool, still looking for their first European trophy. Liverpool won 1–0 at Anfield with a freak goal, and although Martin Peters scored twice at White Hart Lane, Steve Heighway grabbed a goal to put the Reds through on away goals.

Manager Bill Nicholson retired soon after the 1974 UEFA Cup final, marred by crowd violence

UEFA Cup 1973–74

Another League Cup final triumph in a 1–0 win over Norwich gave Nicholson's side the chance to have another crack at Euro glory the following season. Determined to avenge their semi-final defeat at the hands of Liverpool the previous year, Spurs began in emphatic fashion, trouncing Swiss side Grasshoppers of Zurich 9–2 on aggregate.

The second round saw them dispose of Scottish side Aberdeen 5–2 and things began to look ominous for the rest of Europe. Spurs looked unstoppable as they demolished Dynamo Tbilisi 6–2 on aggregate and then saw off German giants Cologne, winning 3–0 at home and 2–1 away.

The semi-final against Locomotiv Leipzig saw Tottenham turn in two brilliant performances. Peters and Ralph Coates scored in the 2–1 win in East Germany while Chivers and teenager Chris McGrath hit the goals in a 2–0 victory at White Hart Lane.

That set up another final against Feyenoord, but it was to be a dark episode in the English club's long and illustrious history. Not only did Spurs lose a final for the first time, going down 2–0 in Holland after drawing 2–2 at home, but rioting fans brought shame on English football and earned the club a European ban. There were 50 arrests and more than 200 people were hurt in Rotterdam as the campaign ended in shame. It was too much for Nicholson, who appealed at half-time for the fighting to stop. He had planned to retire after a third European success and, despite hanging on for a few more months, Nicholson resigned early the following season.

Mike England celebrates his goal in the home leg of the 1974 UEFA Cup final against Feyenoord

The Eighties

If ever a man was ready to follow in the illustrious footsteps of Bill Nicholson it was Keith Burkinshaw, although some pundits claimed that the job was harder than ever before.

Relegated to the second division in 1977, Spurs were at a low ebb. But after guiding them back to the top flight at the first attempt, Burkinshaw added Argentina's 1978 World Cup stars Ossie Ardiles and Ricky Villa to the exceptional home-grown talent of Glenn Hoddle.

The 1981 FA Cup victory over Manchester City put Spurs back in Europe and they returned in impressive fashion with a 6–1 aggregate victory over Dutch masters Ajax, young reserve striker Mark Falco scoring three times.

A tight 2–1 aggregate win over Irish side Dundalk left them paired against Eintracht Frankfurt of Germany in the third round. A vital away goal from Hoddle saw Spurs through 3–2 on aggregate to set up a semi-final against Barcelona.

The Spaniards showed the unpleasant side of their game, and what should have been a clash of two great European clubs turned into a violent and cynical battle. The Spaniards kicked their way towards the final with a 1–1 draw at White Hart Lane in the first leg, after which they were christened the "Butchers of Barcelona" by the press.

The violence was such that a policeman had to intervene when defender Manolo squared up to Graham Roberts, who scored Spurs's equalizer after a mistake

Mark Falco, one of Tottenham's unsung heroes in Europe, scores against Feyenoord in 1983

by Ray Clemence had let Barcelona take the lead. Even though Barcelona were reduced to 10 men in the 57th minute, it was not enough to help Spurs win. The return leg was more memorable for the power failure which knocked out the lights in the Nou Camp Stadium than for the goal from Danish star Allen Simonsen which gave the Spaniards a place in the final.

Cup-winners' Cup 1982–83

A second successive FA Cup victory gave Spurs another chance in the Cup-winners' Cup, but it was short-lived. After beating Irish part-timers Coleraine easily with an aggregate score of 7–0, Spurs fell in the second round to German giants Bayern Munich, who drew 1–1 at White Hart Lane and won 4–1 in thick fog at the Olympic Stadium.

UEFA Cup 1983–84

Spurs qualified for the UEFA Cup after finishing fourth in the League, and the campaign was to end in a spectacular success. Hoddle inspired Spurs to some of their best European performances since the Sixties, particularly the defeat of long-standing enemies Feyenoord.

The Dutch came to White Hart Lane for a second-round tie with a veteran Johan Cruyff and a young Ruud Gullit among their ranks. But Cruyff was sent packing by Hoddle and his men as Spurs revived memories of the glory, glory nights with a

UEFA Cup Final, 1984: Tony Parks saves Gudjohnsen's penalty

UEFA Cup Final

1st leg **9 May 1984**
Anderlecht Stadium, Brussels –
Attendance 38,000

2nd leg **23 May 1984**
White Hart Lane, Tottenham –
Attendance: 46,258

Anderlecht 1
Tottenham Hotspur 1
(Miller)

Tottenham Hotspur 1
(Roberts)
Anderlecht 1
Tottenham won 4-3 on penalties after extra time

Team: Parks, Thomas, Hughton, Roberts, Miller, Perryman, Stevens, (Mabbutt),Archibald, Falco, Hazard, Galvin

Team: Parks, Thomas, Hughton, Roberts, Miller (Ardiles), Mabbutt (Dick), Hazard, Archibald, Stevens, Galvin, Falco

4–2 home win. The first half was perhaps the best 45 minutes of Spurs football since the double era. Hoddle was magnificent as he led Cruyff a merry dance, "nutmegging" him twice as Spurs took a 4–0 lead before half-time. Hoddle had a hand in all four goals, two each going to Tony Galvin and Steve Archibald.

The Dutch reorganized their side and scored two second-half goals to give themselves a chance, but Spurs won the away leg 2–0 to waltz through. The third round saw revenge over Bayern Munich. Despite going down 1–0 in the first leg, Spurs won 2–0 on another great night at White Hart Lane with goals from Archibald and Falco.

A 4–2 aggregate win over Austria Vienna was enough to see Spurs through to the semi-finals against Hajduk Split once again. Although Spurs lost the first leg 2–1, Falco scored an invaluable away goal. When Micky Hazard hit the only goal of the home leg with a wonderful free-kick, Spurs went through to the final on the away goals rule.

The final with Anderlecht was disappointing in terms of pure football, but unforgettably dramatic. Paul Miller's header helped Spurs to a 1–1 draw in the first leg in Brussels, but with Clemence, Hoddle and the suspended Steve Perryman out of the second leg, it was always going to be tight, especially after Anderlecht took an early lead at White Hart Lane.

But in a barnstorming finish, acting captain Graham Roberts led from the front by bundling in a late equalizer to take the game to extra time. No further goals meant that a penalty shoot-out was needed, and it called on the nerve of Tony Parks, standing in for Clemence. The young keeper rose to the occasion, diving to save Arnor Gudjohnsen's final penalty to bring the UEFA Cup back to Tottenham.

For manager Keith Burkinshaw it was a fitting finale and for Spurs and their supporters it was another major European success.

Acting captain Graham Roberts celebrates his dramatic equalizer in the 1984 UEFA Cup Final

Micky Hazard scores from a free kick in the 1984 UEFA Cup semi-final against Hajduk Split

UEFA Cup 1984–85

As holders, Spurs were granted the right to defend the trophy the following year, but could not repeat the feat. Despite hammering Sporting Braga 9–0 on aggregate and seeing off Bruges and Bohemians of Prague, they eventually fell victim to Real Madrid in the quarter-finals, with Perryman scoring an own goal in the first leg and then being sent off in the second.

The Nineties

Tottenham's lack of success on the domestic front has hit them hard in terms of European glory. Only the 1991 FA Cup triumph gave them any European action, but even this was short-lived. Spurs reached the quarter-finals of the Cup-winners' Cup – a competition for which they'd set the standard for English teams to follow when they won it in 1963 – but went no further.

Even with England's second-highest goalscorer in Gary Lineker in their colours, Tottenham could not beat their old adversaries Feyenoord. The qualifying round saw them put out little-known Austrians Sparkasse Stockerau with two 1–0 wins, and then they beat Hajduk Split 2–1 on aggregate, having lost 1–0 away.

The next round brought Porto, who were top of the Portuguese league with one of the best defensive records in Europe at the time. Spurs made a mockery of Porto's reputation with a resounding 3–1 win at White Hart Lane, including a superb goal from Gary Lineker after a five-man move of breathtaking one-touch football.

But once again Feyenoord were waiting to spoil Tottenham's night, and after winning a tight game 1–0 at home in Rotterdam, they held out for a goalless draw in London to go though.

The glory, glory nights at White Hart Lane have been sadly missed by supporters of a team which set the ball rolling in Europe almost 35 years ago now. The 1990s may have delivered little but there is no denying Tottenham's European pedigree. Let's hope a return to those heady nights of the Sixties, Seventies and Eighties is just around the corner…

European Cup-winners' Cup, 1991: Lineker scores the third in Tottenham's 3–1 victory over FC Porto

Spurs in Europe – The Complete Record

First Round	Second Round	Third Round	Quarter-Final	Semi-Final	Final
1961–62 European Cup					
vs. Gornik Zabrze (Poland) **a** L 2–4 (Jones, Dyson) **h** W 8–1 (Blanchflower pen, Jones 3, Smith 2, Dyson, White)	vs. Feyenoord (Holland) (a) W 3–1 (Dyson, Saul 2) (h) D 1–1 (Dyson)	vs. Dukla Prague (Czechoslovakia) (a) L 0–1 (h) W 4–1 (Smith 2, Mackay 2)		vs. Benfica (Portugal) (a) L 1–3 (Smith) (h) W 2–1 (Smith, Blanchflower pen)	
1962–63 European Cup-winners' Cup					
First Round Bye	vs. Glasgow Rangers (Scotland) (h) W 5–2 (Norman, White 2, Allen, Shearer og). (a) W 3–2 (Greaves, Smith 2)	vs. Slovan Bratislava (Czechoslovakia) (a) L 0–2 (h) W 6–0 (Mackay, Greaves 2, Smith, Jones, White)		vs. OFK Belgrade (Yugoslavia) (a) W 2–1 (Dyson, White) (h) W 3–1 (Jones, Smith, Mackay)	Final (in Rotterdam) vs. Atletico Madrid (Spain) W 5–1 (Dyson 2, Greaves 2, White)
1963–64 European Cup-winners' Cup					
vs. Manchester United (England) (h) W 2–0 (Mackay, Dyson) (a) L 1–4 (Greaves)					
1967–68 – European Cup-winners' Cup					
vs. Hajduk Split (Yugoslavia) (a) W 2–0 (Robertson, Greaves) (h) W 4–3 (Robertson 2, Gilzean, Venables)	vs. Olympique Lyonnais (France) (a) L 0–1 (h) W 4–3 (Greaves 2, Venables, Jones)				
1971–72 UEFA Cup					
vs. Keflavik (Iceland) (a) W 6–1 (Gilzean 3, Coates, Mullery 2) (h) W 9–0 (Chivers 3, Perryman, Coates, Knowles, Gilzean 2, Holder)	vs. Nantes (France) (a) D 0–0 (h) W 1–0 (Peters)	vs. Rapid Bucharest (Romania) (h) W 3–0 (Peters, Chivers 2) (a) W 2–0 (Pearce, Chivers)	vs. UT Arad (USSR) (a) W 2–0 (Morgan, England) (h) D 1–1 (Gilzean)	vs. AC Milan (Italy) (h) W 2–1 (Perryman 2) (a) D 1–1 (Mullery)	vs. Wolves (England) (a) W 2–1 (Chivers 2) (h) D 1–1 (Mullery)
1972–73 UEFA Cup					
vs. Lyn Oslo (Norway) (a) W 6–3 (Pratt, Chivers 2, Gilzean 2, Peters) (h) W 6–0 (Chivers 3, Pearce, Coates 2)	vs. Olympiakos Piraeus (Greece) (h) W 4–0 (Chivers, Coates, Pearce 2) (a) L 0–1	vs. Red Star Belgrade (Yugoslavia) (h) W 2–0 (Chivers, Gilzean) (a) L 0–1	vs. Vitoria Setubal (Portugal) (h) W 1–0 (Evans) (a) L 1–2 (Chivers)	vs. Liverpool (England) (a) L 0–1 (h) W 2–1 (Peters 2)	
1973–74 UEFA Cup					
vs. Grasshoppers Zurich (Switzerland) (a) W 5–1 (Gilzean 2, Chivers 2, Evans) (h) W 4–1 (Lador og, Peters 2, England)	vs. Aberdeen (Scotland) (a) D 1–1 (Coates) (h) W 4–1 (McGrath 2, Neighbour, Peters)	vs. Dinamo Tbilisi (USSR) (a) D 1–1 (Coates) (h) W 5–1 (Chivers 2, Peters 2, McGrath)	vs. Cologne (W Germany) (a) W 2–1 (Peters, McGrath) (h) W 3–0 (Peters, Coates, Chivers)	vs. Locomotiv Leipzig (East Germany) (a) W 2–1 (Peters, Coates) (h) W 2–0 (McGrath, Chivers)	vs. Feyenoord (Holland) (h) D 2–2 (England, Van Daele og) (a) L 0–2
1981–82 European Cup-winners' Cup					
vs. Ajax Amsterdam (Holland) (a) W 3–1 (Villa, Falco 2) (h) W 3–0 (Ardiles, Galvin, Falco)	vs. Dundalk (Ireland) (a) D 1–1 (Crooks) (h) W 1–0 (Crooks)	vs. Eintracht Frankfurt (W Germany) (h) W 2–0 (Miller, Hazard) (a) L 1–2 (Hoddle)		vs. Barcelona (Spain) (h) D 1–1 (Roberts) (a) L 0–1	
1982–83 European Cup-winners' Cup					
vs. Coleraine (Ireland) (a) W 3–0 (Archibald, Crooks 2) (h) W 4–0 (Brooke, Mabbutt, Crooks, Gibson)	vs. Bayern Munich (W Germany) (h) D 1–1 (Archibald) (a) L 1–4 (Hughton)				
1983–84 UEFA Cup					
vs. Drogheda (Ireland) (a) W 6–0 (Mabbutt 2, Falco 2, Crooks, Galvin) (h) W 8–0 (Hughton, Roberts 2, Brazil 2, Falco 2, Archibald)	vs. Feyenoord (Holland) (h) W 4–2 (Galvin 2, Archibald 2) (a) W 2–0 (Hughton, Galvin)	vs. Bayern Munich (W Germany) (a) L 1–0 (h) W 2–0 (Archibald, Falco)	vs. Austria Vienna (Austria) (h) W 2–0 (Archibald, Brazil) (a) D 2–2 (Ardiles, Brazil)	vs. Hajduk Split (Yugoslavia) (a) L 1–2 (Falco) (h) W 1–0 (Hazard)	vs. Anderlecht (Belgium) (a) D 1–1 (Miller) (h) D 1–1 (Roberts) Spurs won 4–3 on penalties aet
1984–85 UEFA Cup					
vs. Sporting Braga (Portugal) (a) W 3–0 (Falco 2, Galvin) (h) W 6–0 (Crooks 3, Stevens, Hughton, Falco)	vs. Bruges (Belgium) (a) L 1–2 (Allen) (h) W 3–0 (Roberts, Allen, Hazard)	vs. Bohemians Prague (Czechoslovakia) (h) W 2–0 (Stevens, Ondra og) (a) D 1–1 (Falco)	vs. Real Madrid (Spain) (h) L 0–1 (a) D 0–0		

Qualifying Round	First Round		Second Round		Third Round
1991–92 European Cup-winners' Cup					
vs. Sparkasse Stockerau (Austria) (a) W 1–0 (Durie) (h) W 1–0 (Mabbutt)	vs. Hajduk Split (Yugoslavia) (a) L 0–1 (h) W 2–0 (Durie, Tuttle)		vs. FC Porto (Portugal) (h) W 3–1 (Lineker 2, Durie) (a) D 0–0		vs. Feyenoord (Holland) (a) L 0–1 (h) D 0–0

Chapter 4
Up For The Cup

Spurs and the Cup go together like eggs and bacon or bangers and mash. Here we look at some of the great Cup triumphs from Tottenham's history

Early triumphs

THERE has always been a special relationship between Tottenham Hotspur and Cup football, and never more so than at the start of a decade. Since the turn of the century, Spurs have had a habit of winning something when the year ends in a '1'.

To the FA Cup wins of 1901, 1921, 1961, 1981 and 1991 can be added the League Championships of 1951 and 1961 as well as their League Cup triumph of 1971. Spurs also won the League Cup in 1973, as well as further FA Cups in 1962, 1967 and 1982, to make them the game's Cup specialists.

Having equalled Aston Villa's record of seven FA Cup wins in 1982, it was not until 1996 that Manchester United overtook them to set a new record of nine FA Cup triumphs. However much Spurs might be struggling in the League, they have always seemed to raise themselves for the Cup, and in the last 35 years Wembley has been like a second home to the team from White Hart Lane.

Tottenham's remarkable Cup record began as far back as 1901, and some of the records set during that famous Cup run have never been beaten. It was also notable for a number of firsts: Spurs were the first southern professional side to win the Cup; the first and only non-League side to win it since the Football League was founded in 1888 and the first London side with a truly working-class support to reach the final.

Little wonder that a record crowd of 114,815 turned up to watch that final against Sheffield United. It was the first game in world football to attract a crowd of more than 100,000 and is still the third-highest attendance in English football, behind the 1923 and 1913 Cup finals.

The Cup run had begun at Preston, who had completed the first ever League and Cup Double in 1897 and beaten Spurs in 1900. So there was some consternation when Spurs drew the men from Deepdale again the following year. Preston took an early lead in the first game at White Hart Lane but Sandy Brown scored a late equalizer to force a replay. Spurs wasted no time in seeing off Preston in the replay, roared on by a large band of travelling fans. Their 4–2 win included a hat-trick from Sandy Brown, and landed them a second-round meeting with Cup-holders Bury.

Once again Spurs fell behind, but Brown came to the rescue, scoring twice to take his tally to six goals in three games. Spurs were in the quarter-finals for only the second time and they beat Reading after a replay to set up their first-ever semi-final, against Midlands giants West Bromwich.

Once again it was Brown's day as he scored all four goals in a thumping 4–0 win over the mighty League side. Spurs were in their first FA Cup final, to be

Cup Final, 1961: Terry Dyson beats the great Gordon Banks to complete a 2–0 win over Leicester City

played at Crystal Palace against Sheffield United. Once again Sandy Brown had to equalize after Spurs conceded an early goal, and the Scotsman scored again before Spurs fell victim to one of the most controversial goals in the history of the Cup. Goalkeeper George Clawley failed to hold a shot and United forward William Bennett forced the ball over the goal-line. Bennett claimed a corner, which the linesman signalled, but the referee awarded a goal, claiming later that he thought the ball had crossed the line. Unfortunately for him, the game was the first Cup final to be filmed, and footage released a week later showed the ball was at least a foot from the line.

Spurs gained revenge in the replay at Bolton's Burnden Park when the remarkable Brown scored his 15th goal of that Cup run to cap a 3–1 win. That total of 15 goals, scored in just seven games, set a new record for the competition that is unlikely ever to be beaten. It was a historic win for Spurs, and the start of a long association with the FA Cup, still the most famous club competition in world football.

Tottenham's next FA Cup triumph came 20 years later. No southern side had won it in the intervening years, but Spurs were to change that. They destroyed Bristol Rovers, Bradford City and Southend in the early rounds before drawing Cup-holders Aston Villa, a game which drew a then-record crowd of 51,991 to White Hart Lane. The home fans were rewarded when Jimmy Banks scored the only goal of the game to beat Villa and put Spurs into the semi-finals.

Bert Bliss scored twice in the semi-final at Hillsborough to see off Preston once again and set up a final against Wolves at Stamford Bridge. Another big crowd of 72,805 set a new world record for receipts, and saw Spurs win through the only goal of the game, scored by left-winger Jimmy Dimmock early in the second half. Having started a run from the halfway line, Dimmock took advantage of a lucky deflection and cut into the penalty area, ignoring better-placed team-mates, to hammer home the decisive goal.

Spurs had won the Cup again, but it was to be a long wait before their next triumph.

The Sixties

Although Spurs had won the FA Cup in 1901 and 1921, it was in the 60s that they established their reputation as a great Cup side. The year of the Double is obviously the one that will always have a special place in the hearts of all Tottenham supporters, but the triumphs of 1962 and 1967 cannot be forgotten.

By the time Spurs started their FA Cup run in January 1961, they were well on the way to the League title. They started with a difficult tie at Charlton in the third round. Nearly 60,000 people packed into The Valley to see Tottenham win 3–2, with two goals from Les Allen and one from Terry Dyson.

The next round saw Spurs paired with Crewe Alexandra, but there was to be no repeat of the previous year's embarrassment when humble Crewe had held Spurs to a 2–2 draw at Gresty Road before being blown away 13–2 at White Hart Lane. This time Spurs made sure first time around with a 5–1 win, the goals shared among Dyson, Allen, Dave Mackay, Bobby Smith and Cliff Jones.

The fifth round took Spurs to Villa Park, their unlucky FA Cup ground where they'd lost three semi-finals in the space of eight years. But with Mackay outstanding and Jones on song again, Spurs won 2–0. The fans now scented the Double, and the quarter-final against Sunderland had an excited buzz about it. The away leg saw Cup-specialist Jones grab an all-important goal in a 1–1 draw. A fantastic display in the replay saw the Rokerites thumped 5–0, with Dyson grabbing two and Mackay, Smith and Allen getting the other goals.

The semi-final was perhaps the most worrying game of the campaign, not just because the opponents were reigning League champions Burnley but because the game was back at Villa Park, scene of those semi-final defeats in 1948, 1953 and 1956. But the hoodoo was laid to rest as two goals from Smith and one from Jones saw Tottenham run out 3–0 winners.

And so to Spurs' first-ever appearance at Wembley, where Leicester City were to provide the opposition. The League title was already in the bag and the precious Double was only 90 minutes away. Strangely, the match itself was something of a disappointment after the intense build-up. Leicester full-back Len Chalmers was injured in the 19th minute and, as this was in the pre-substitute era, hobbled about for the rest of the game. It wasn't until the 67th minute that Bobby Smith put Spurs ahead, thumping a shot past a young Gordon Banks in the Leicester goal. Smith then crossed for Dyson to head home 10 minutes later and the Double was complete for the first time this century.

Spurs had obviously enjoyed their Wembley day out because 12 months later they were back again. The Cup run saw Birmingham City defeated after a replay in the third round, with new signing Jimmy Greaves on target in both games. Plymouth were hammered 5–1 in the fourth round and then West Brom were beaten 4–2 in the fifth, with Greaves and Smith scoring twice.

Spurs drew Aston Villa again, this time at home, and beat them 2–0 to set up a cracking semi-final against Manchester United at Hillsborough. Matt Busby's men had no answer as goals from Jones, Terry Medwin and Greaves put Spurs into their second final in

Bobby Smith, (left) Danny Blanchflower (centre) and Jimmy Greaves celebrate after scoring the goals which sank Burnley 3–1 in the 1962 FA Cup final

Cyril Knowles, Terry Venables, Joe Kinnear and goalscorer Jimmy Robertson celebrate the 1967 FA Cup win over Chelsea, the first all-London final

succession, as Spurs went marching on.

Burnley, who had been fighting it out with Tottenham and Ipswich for the League, were the opponents at Wembley. Greaves kept up his phenomenal record with an early goal, and although Burnley equalized, another Bobby Smith goal and a Danny Blanchflower penalty brought the Cup back to White Hart Lane.

By the time Spurs won the FA Cup again, most of the Double team had gone. Greaves, Mackay and Jones were the only survivors as a new generation tasted success for the first time.

Alan Gilzean scored to see off Millwall in a third-round replay, and the Scot scored twice along with Greaves as Portsmouth were beaten 3–1 in the next round. A double by Greaves knocked out Bristol City to set up a quarter-final clash with Birmingham City. A scoreless draw at St Andrews was followed up with an incredible 6–0 hammering at White Hart Lane, which saw Terry Venables and Greaves on the double, with Frank Saul and Gilzean getting the other goals.

The semi-final saw Tottenham pitted against Nottingham Forest, but goals by Greaves and Saul saw them off to set up the first all-London final, with Chelsea providing the opposition.

The 2–1 final scoreline hardly reflected the ease with which Spurs won. Goals by Scottish winger Jimmy Robertson and Saul either side of half-time were scant reward for their domination, and Chelsea's goal five minutes from the end was little consolation.

League Cup Success – the Seventies

Like most big clubs, Tottenham did not pay too much attention to the League Cup when it was first introduced in the early 1960s. It was not until 1967 when the final was moved to Wembley (rather than being played on a home-and-away basis), that it became interesting. The addition of a UEFA Cup place in 1971 gave the trophy greater weight. With so much more at stake, the bigger clubs gave it more prominence, though it could be argued this trend has been reversed recently with the withdrawal of a UEFA Cup place.

Spurs entered for the first time in 1966–67 but fell at the first hurdle to West Ham. Two years later they reached the semi-finals, only to be beaten by arch-rivals Arsenal over two bad-tempered legs. Arsenal were to get their come-uppance at Wembley in the final when third-division Swindon beat them 3–1.

So it was with some trepidation that Spurs approached their first final two years later, also against third-division opposition in the shape of Aston Villa.

It was the beginning of Bill Nicholson's second successful era and came after he had sold the great Jimmy

Martin Chivers in typical goalscoring style. The powerful centre-forward clinched Tottenham's first League Cup with both goals in the 2–0 win over Aston Villa in 1971

Greaves. Nicholson used Greaves as bait to lure Martin Peters from West Ham. With a young Steve Perryman and the dependable Alan Mullery, Spurs had the midfield to provide ammunition for Martin Chivers and Alan Gilzean in attack. With Pat Jennings blossoming into the country's best goalkeeper, and Mike England dominating alongside Phil Beal, Cyril knowles and Joe Kinnear in defence, Spurs had a strong side – as a tally of three trophies in two years was about to prove.

The 1971 Cup run started with a 3–0 win over lowly Swansea, with goals from Peters, Perryman and winger Roger Morgan. Another young winger, Jimmy Pearce, scored in the next round as Sheffield United were beaten 2–1, with Chivers scoring the other goal. Peters hit a hat-trick and Alan Gilzean got two as West Bromwich were hammered 5–0 in the next round, and the fifth round saw Gilzean strike again to add to Chivers's treble as Coventry were thumped 4–1. There was suddenly a real feeling that Tottenham could take the trophy to White Hart Lane.

In the two-legged semi-final Tottenham had to leave home for the first time in the competition, travelling to second-division Bristol City for a 1–1 draw. The second leg at White Hart Lane was an epic battle, with Tottenham finally winning 2–0 in extra time through goals by Chivers and Pearce.

Spurs were through to their first League Cup final at Wembley, which had been a happy hunting-ground for third-division teams over the years with Queens Park Rangers winning in 1967 and Swindon's famous win over Arsenal in 1968.

Villa made Spurs work for every ball before the latter's class eventually shone through. It was not until the 78th minute that Spurs scored, and not surprisingly Chivers made the breakthrough. The big striker had just made his England debut after a prolific season, and his confidence showed when he rammed home a rebound after Pearce's shot was blocked. Three minutes later Chivers scored a wonderful solo goal, running through the Villa defence before scoring with a low shot. It was Tottenham's first League Cup final triumph, but it was not long before they became the first side to win it twice.

In the 1973 run, Huddersfield were the first victims as they went down 2–1, with Gilzean and Chivers scoring the goals. That was followed by a tough battle against Middlesbrough, managed by Jack Charlton and led by former Spurs youngster Graeme Souness. It took three games to see Boro off after a hard-fought

Spurs rejoice at their second League Cup win in two years, after Ralph Coates's goal gave them a 1–0 win over Norwich in 1973

1–1 draw at Ayresome Park followed by a tense scoreless game at White Hart Lane. Spurs finally triumphed 2–1 in the second replay.

Goals from Perryman and Peters saw off Millwall in the next round to set up a tough quarter-final against Liverpool. Jennings was outstanding as Spurs held on at Anfield for a 1–1 draw, with Martin Peters scoring the precious goal. Back at White Hart Lane, Spurs won the replay 3–1 in a thrilling display, with Chivers scoring twice and John Pratt netting a third. This set up a semi-final clash against Wolverhampton Wanderers, whom Spurs had beaten over two legs in the previous year's enthralling UEFA Cup final.

Again it was a close tie. Pratt and Peters were on target in a 2–1 win at Molineux, but the second leg was nerve-racking and it took every ounce of Spurs' character to come through unscathed. Wolves forced the game into extra time as they led 2–1 after 90 minutes, but another Chivers goal meant that Spurs were through to a Wembley showdown with second-division Norwich.

Unfortunately the decider was to be no Wembley thriller, although Ralph Coates will always remember it for the low shot he drilled home in the 72nd minute. The winger never really fulfilled his promise after Nicholson spent a British record £180,000 to sign him from Burnley. But after going on as substitute at Wembley, Coates livened up what turned out to be a disappointing match with the game's only goal and ensured his place in Tottenham's history.

The Eighties

IN TERMS of sheer excitement and drama, the 1981 FA Cup final replay will be remembered as one of the greatest games seen at Wembley.

Keith Burkinshaw had patiently built an entertaining and attacking side, combining the home-grown talents of Glenn Hoddle with the South American skills of Ricky Villa and Ossie Ardiles. It may have culminated in the greatest goal ever seen in an FA Cup final, but the 1981 Cup run started in far less spectacular style, and far more mundane surroundings.

It began on a grey January afternoon against London rivals QPR. The game at Loftus Road was a drab affair that ended scoreless, but Tottenham showed their intentions in the replay by winning 3–1 with goals from Hoddle, Tony Galvin and new striker Garth Crooks. His prolific strike partner was the moody Scotsman Steve Archibald, who scored a late goal after Garry Brooke's opener to sink a stubborn Hull side 2–0 in the next round.

Archibald scored again, along with Ardiles and Chris Hughton, in a comfortable 3–1 home win over Coventry that set up a quarter-final date with Exeter. The third-division side had already beaten Newcastle and Leicester, and put up a good show before defenders Paul Miller and Graham Roberts scored in the second half to end their resistance.

The semi-final against Wolves was a classic, with a hotly-disputed late penalty at Hillsborough earning the Midlands side a 2–2 draw. But the replay at Highbury brought a taste of things to come. Spurs were fired up and two first-half goals from Garth Crooks, the second set up by a superb pass from Hoddle, put Spurs in control before Ricky Villa finished it off with a swerving shot from 35 yards.

Spurs were back at Wembley to face Manchester City in the 100th FA Cup final. The first game was a drab affair, though, with City taking a 29th-minute lead through Tommy Hutchinson. The Scottish winger then earned the dubious distinction of scoring for both sides when he deflected a free kick from Hoddle into his own net – and it was enough to earn Tottenham a replay.

Villa had been substituted during the first game, and cried as he thought his chance of FA Cup glory was gone; but Burkinshaw assured him he would be in for the replay – and what a decision that turned out to be.

The replay – the first at Wembley – was one of the best games in FA Cup history. Villa

The best Cup goal ever? Ricky Villa weaves through Manchester City's defence in the final minutes of the 1981 FA Cup Final replay

gave Spurs the lead as early as the eighth minute but three minutes later Steve Mackenzie struck a beautiful equalizer. A Kevin Reeves penalty gave City the lead five minutes after half time, but 10 minutes later Garth Crooks made it 2–2. Then, with time running out, Villa received the ball wide on the left before going on a mazy, jinking run that saw him weave his way through the City defence before sliding the ball into the net. It was a beautiful goal and a worthy winner, leading to celebrations all over London that went on long into the night.

The following year was the club's centenary and they celebrated with another FA Cup win, although the final could never match the drama or excitement of 12 months earlier.

The third-round opponents were bitter rivals Arsenal, and it was an uncharacteristic mistake by former Tottenham goalkeeper Pat Jennings that let Crooks in for the game's only goal. Crooks repeated the feat to sink Leeds at home in the next round, and then a single goal from Mark Falco saw off Aston Villa.

Spurs were drawn away in the quarter-final but still did not leave London, beating Chelsea 3–2 at Stamford Bridge with Hoddle in devastating form.

Leicester were the semi-final opponents, but they were beaten 2–0 with a goal from Garth Crooks and an own goal from Ian Wilson. It was to be Ardiles' last game for Spurs for six months, as he returned to Argentina and then went to France while Britain and Argentina fought over the Falkland Islands.

Villa was also missing as Spurs took on second-division QPR, managed by Terry Venables, in what turned out to be a dour final. Although Hoddle scored with 10 minutes of extra time remaining, Rangers equalised in the dying moments though Terry Fenwick, later to become a Spurs player.

For the second year running Tottenham needed a replay to win the Cup, and the game's decisive goal was scored by Hoddle from the penalty spot after Roberts was upended in the sixth minute. It was hardly a stylish win, but it put Spurs level with Aston Villa as the only clubs to have won the FA Cup seven times.

Glenn Hoddle scores the penalty that won the FA Cup in 1982, making Spurs the first side to retain it since they had done so 20 years earlier

The Eighties – the Nineties

1987 was almost a great year for Spurs in both domestic Cup competitions – but not quite.

David Pleat had been appointed manager in the summer of 1986 and introduced a new style by playing five men in midfield with Clive Allen up-front as a lone striker. Although the style of play suited the players and proved highly entertaining, it ultimately failed to provide any trophies.

That year's League Cup semifinal was a classic. Having sent Barnsley, Birmingham, Cambridge and West Ham packing, the latter with a 5–0 win, Spurs faced the old enemy full of confidence. Allen scored in a 1–0 win at Highbury and then put Spurs ahead in the second leg. But Arsenal pulled back two goals to set up a replay, which was again at White Hart Lane.

Once again, Allen scored for Spurs, but again Arsenal equalized and David Rocastle hit the decisive goal with only five minutes remaining, the first time the Gunners had been ahead in the tie.

But Spurs went one better in the FA Cup. After beating Scunthorpe, Crystal Palace and Newcastle, Spurs faced Wimbledon in the quarter-finals. Goals from Chris Waddle and Hoddle put Spurs into a semi-final against Watford, who were destroyed 4–1 in a one-sided game at Villa Park.

With Spurs in confident mood and Allen in hot form, they were firm favourites to beat Coventry in the final. True to form, Allen scored after only two minutes for his 49th goal of the season, but Coventry equalized soon afterwards. Gary Mabbutt restored the lead on the stroke of half-time, but Keith Houchen took the game into extra time with a diving header. Mabbutt then repeated Tommy Hutchinson's feat of six years earlier when he scored an own goal, the ball flying off his boot and over goalkeeper Ray Clemence

Clive Allen celebrates his opening goal in the 1987 FA Cup final, his 49th of a memorable season. But his joy was to turn to misery

for Coventry's winner. It had been a superb final but the wrong result for Spurs, and their first defeat in eight FA Cup finals.

But Mabbutt was back just four years later to lift the Cup as captain. The 1991 win was a triumph of will over adversity and owed most to Paul Gascoigne. Spurs were deep in financial trouble, and while manager Terry Venables spent most of the season trying to put together a rescue package, Gascoigne was coming to the rescue on the field.

It was his free kick that allowed Paul Stewart to score the goal that sank Blackpool in the third round. Gazza was again in brilliant form against Oxford in

1991 FA Cup semi-final: Paul Gascoigne's goal from a 30-yard free kick has Arsenal in trouble

Tragedy: Crucial ligament damage from this rash tackle on Gary Charles put Gazza's career on hold

the fourth round, scoring two superb goals and making two more as Tottenham won 4–2. Gascoigne again made the difference at Portsmouth, scoring both goals as Spurs came from behind to win 2–1. He then finished off Notts County in the quarter-final with a superb late winner.

But the next game was the big one – Arsenal against Spurs at Wembley, the first FA Cup semi-final to be played beneath the Twin Towers. Arsenal were on the brink of wrapping up the League title and were looking for the Double when the two sides clashed, but Gazza had other ideas. With only five minutes gone, Spurs were awarded a free kick fully 30 yards from goal. Gascoigne surprised everybody by running up to shoot from long range, and his audacity paid off when his effort flew into the top corner of David Seaman's net. Four minutes later Gascoigne sent Paul Allen away on the right to set up Gary Lineker for a second. Spurs were in control – and Arsenal were in shock. Although Alan Smith pulled a goal back and the less-than-fit Gascoigne had to retire through exhaustion, Lineker scored again to complete a memorable 3–1 victory.

The final against Nottingham Forest should have been a showpiece for Gascoigne's wonderful talents, and his swansong before departing for Lazio in Italy, but it ended up as one of the blackest days of his career, even though Tottenham won the Cup.

The first sign of trouble was a high tackle into the chest of Garry Parker after 90 seconds. Had Gascoigne been booked then, he might have calmed down, but he wasn't and he didn't. Then 10 minutes later, with Gary Charles dribbling the ball across the penalty box, Gascoigne flew into a rash tackle and collapsed in agony. He was carried off with severed cruciate ligaments and his career would never be the same again.

To add insult to injury, Stuart Pearce belted in the ensuing free kick though a gap in the wall created by a shove on the Spurs defenders. Everything looked to be going wrong. Lineker scored midway though the first half but was given offside – wrongly, as television replays showed. Five minutes later Lineker's luck was really out as he had a penalty saved by Mark Crossley after the Forest goalkeeper had pulled him down.

But Spurs kept going and Paul Stewart finally hit an equalizer to take the game into extra time. Mabbutt had sweet revenge for his misfortune four years earlier when he pressured Forest defender Des Walker into heading the ball into his own net to give the Cup to Tottenham for a record eighth time.

The Premiership Stars

Chapter 5

Every fan has a favourite, and here we present 18 of the best and most popular Spurs players from the club's first five years in the Premiership.

Paul **Allen**

Paul Allen will forever be remembered for becoming the youngest-ever Wembley FA Cup finalist when, at just 17 years and 256 days, he played for West Ham in their 1980 triumph over Arsenal. After former Spurs defender Willie Young tripped him up just as he was about to go through and score a fairytale goal at Wembley, the football authorities showed as much emotion as the watching public by making the "professional foul" a sending-off offence.

But Allen did a lot more in his career than instigate a rule change. His collection of 23 England Youth caps is still a record, and he became a hugely-popular player at White Hart Lane during a mostly-barren period for the club. Having started at West Ham, he moved to Spurs in June 1985 for £400,000.

Honest, hard-working and a true professional, Paul Allen was often an unsung hero during his eight seasons at White Hart Lane

Paul ALLEN

Born:
28/8/62
Birthplace:
Aveley
Height:
5ft 7in
Weight:
11st 4lb
Signed For Spurs:
19/6/85 for £400,000
Spurs debut:
17/8/85 vs. Watford
Career:
West Ham 1979–85;
Spurs 1985–93(377
apps., 28 goals);
Southampton 1993–95;
Swindon Town 1995–96.
Honours:
3 England U-21 caps,
23 Youth caps, FA Cup-
winner 1980 & '91
Div. 2 champions 1996

A nephew of former Spurs striker Les, Paul was joined at White Hart Lane a year later by his cousin Clive. The pair played in the FA Cup final defeat to Coventry in 1987, but Paul had the consolation of a winners' medal when Spurs beat Nottingham Forest in 1991.

Two years later he was sold to Southampton and then moved to Swindon. An honest and tireless competitor, Paul was frequently an unsung hero during his eight years with Spurs.

Darren **Anderton**

Injury problems have seriously hampered Darren Anderton's Tottenham and England career, but he has proved his ability at the very highest level and is one of Spurs' finest players of recent years.

A series of groin problems have limited his appearances for club and country since he first established himself as one of the best young players in England during the 1993–94 season. Ironically he arrived at the club with a hernia problem after being signed from Portsmouth in 1992, and his career has been punctuated by injury problems ever since.

Anderton made his name at Pompey as a leggy teenager and a key member of the side's run to the FA Cup semi-finals, taking Liverpool

Darren ANDERTON

Born:
3 March 1972
Birthplace:
Southampton
Height:
6ft 1in
Weight:
12st 5lb
Signed For Spurs:
3/6/92 for £1.75m
Spurs debut:
15 August 1992 vs.
Southampton
Career:
Portsmouth 1990–92;
Spurs 1992–present
(159 apps., 28 goals)
Honours:
16 England caps,
12 U-21 caps,
1 U-19 cap

Though dogged by injury, Darren Anderton has earned a name as one of the most exciting players in the Premiership and is an England regular

to a replay and penalties before losing.

After just one-and-a-half seasons in the Portsmouth team, during which he scored 13 goals from the wing, Terry Venables paid £1.75 million to bring the then 20-year-old Anderton to White Hart Lane.

He made a slow start, but once his hernia was operated on there was no stopping him. He linked superbly with Teddy Sheringham and Nick Barmby as Spurs reached the FA Cup semi-finals before losing to Arsenal. When Spurs lost again at that stage, to Everton in 1995, it was Anderton's third losing semi-final, and worse was to follow as England were knocked out of Euro '96 by Germany, his fourth semi-final defeat in five years.

But Anderton had done well to play in all five England matches during the European Championship, having played just nine games in the

1995–96 season after undergoing two groin operations. He struggled again in the 1996–97 season, with another hernia operation in October and then damaged knee ligaments shortly after returning to action.

Another return to fitness was hampered by a persistent hamstring problem that ended his season early. It means that Anderton took no part in Glenn Hoddle's first year in charge of England, although he is still in the manager's plans as one of the most creative players in the country.

One of the best crossers of a ball in the Premiership and superb at beating his marker, Anderton is an excellent passer and can score spectacular goals from long range. He has moved in from the wing to become a central midfielder, and could become a key playmaker for both Spurs and England if he can finally overcome his injury problems.

Chris **Armstrong**

Gerry Francis broke the club's transfer record when he signed Chris Armstrong for £4.5 million from Crystal Palace as Jürgen Klinsmann's replacement in June 1995.

Many thought such a daunting task would be beyond a player who had yet to prove himself a consistent goalscorer in the top flight, but he rose to the challenge and after a slow start passed with flying colours.

Having waited ten League games for his first Premiership goal, he then showed his worth by scoring 22 times in a 46-goal partnership with Teddy Sheringham in the 1995–96 season.

Armstrong was born in Newcastle but grew up in north Wales and was working part-time spraying buses when local side Wrexham signed him on a free transfer from non-League side Llay Welfare in 1989.

When Millwall decided to sell Sheringham to

Chris ARMSTRONG
Born:
19 June 1971
Birthplace:
Newcastle
Height:
6ft 0in
Weight:
12st 10lb
Signed For Spurs:
30/6/95 for £4.5 million
Spurs debut:
19 August 1995 vs. Manchester City
Career:
Wrexham 1988–91; Millwall 1991–92; Crystal Palace 1992–95; Spurs 1995–present (60 apps., 28 goals)
Honours:
1 England "B" cap, Division One Championship 1994.

Fast, powerful and a prolific goalscorer, Chris Armstrong soon filled the void left by the departure of Jurgen Klinsmann in 1995

Nottingham Forest in 1991, they signed Armstrong from Wrexham for £50,000 as his replacement. After only one full season at The Den, in which he scored just five goals and spent most of the time on the substitutes' bench, Crystal Palace paid £1 million for him. They had not replaced Ian Wright after his move to Arsenal almost a year earlier, and saw Armstrong as the answer.

Many people thought it was an excessive fee for an untried player, but he responded with 15 goals in 35 games. It was not enough to prevent Palace going down to the first division, but Armstrong led them straight back up as champions, scoring 23 goals.

The following season he scored only eight goals in the Premiership but scored ten times in cup competitions as Palace reached the semi-finals of both major domestic trophies. His cause was not helped by testing positively for cannabis midway through the season.

He had already won an England "B" cap and looked to be on the verge of a call-up to the full England squad after his successful first season at Spurs, but an ankle injury in August 1996 led to an operation before Christmas that kept him out for the rest of the season.

Exceptionally quick and strong, he is a superb header of the ball and has a powerful right foot. If he can continue to improve on his left foot and put his injury problems behind him, Armstrong could be back in the international reckoning again.

Nick **Barmby**

Nick Barmby's imaginative style was like a breath of fresh air when he burst on to the Premiership scene as a teenager in the 1992–93 season

Nick Barmby was one of a crop of outstanding graduates from the FA's national School of Excellence at Lilleshall to complete his footballing education through the ranks at Tottenham before bursting on to the scene in 1992.

Like Ian Walker, Darren Caskey and Sol Campbell, Barmby emerged as a shining example of the excellent youth policy at White Hart Lane when he became a first-team regular at the age of 18.

Linking up with Teddy Sheringham to superb effect, Barmby scored nine goals in 17 starts that season and captured the country's imagination. He continued to score goals the following year despite having surgery because of shin splints. When he made an England debut as a member of Ossie Ardiles' Famous Five in 1994, his future as an international star looked assured.

But since leaving Spurs in the summer of 1995, things have not gone so well. The Hull-born youngster was homesick for the North and Gerry Francis reluctantly sold him to Middlesbrough for £5.25 million, the first of many big signings by Bryan Robson.

He made a good start at Middlesbrough, but when Brazilian superstar Juninho arrived a few months later the pair failed to click and within a year Barmby moved on to Everton for £5.75 million.

He has struggled to establish himself as a first-team regular at Goodison Park and has since lost his place in the England squad, despite scoring goals against China and Moldova and appearing as a substitute in the European Championship.

A lively and unorthodox forward who has modelled his style on his hero Peter Beardsley, Barmby will need to recapture the form he showed at Spurs if he is to fulfil his massive potential and become an England regular.

Nick BARMBY

Born:
11 February 1974
Birthplace:
Hull
Height:
5ft 7in
Weight:
11st 3lb
Signed For Spurs:
From trainee 9/4/91
Spurs debut:
27 September 1992 vs. Sheffield Wednesday
Career:
Spurs 1991–95 (108 app., 27 goals); Middlesbrough 1995–96; Everton 1996–present
Honours:
9 England caps,
1 "B" cap,
3 U-21 caps,
4 U-19 caps,
7 Youth caps,
9 Schoolboy caps

Colin **Calderwood**

Colin CALDERWOOD

Born:
20 January 1965
Birthplace:
Glasgow
Height:
6ft
Weight:
13st
Signed For Spurs:
22/7/93 for £1.25m
Spurs debut:
14 August 1993 vs.
Newcastle United
Career:
Mansfield Town
1981–85;
Swindon Town 1985–93;
Spurs 1993–present:
(152 apps., 2 goals)
Honours:
Scotland 21 caps,
Division 4
Championship 1986

Colin Calderwood has come a long way from playing in the old fourth division with Mansfield and Swindon. The powerful central defender has become a fixture for both Spurs and Scotland after spending most of his career outside the top flight.

As a Scotsman growing up in Stranraer, it seems incredible that Calderwood did not play a senior game in his native country until he made his home debut for Scotland in 1996.

He joined Mansfield from school and spent four years with the Midlanders before moving to Swindon for £30,000 in 1985. He had immediate success by winning the fourth division title with Swindon in his first season. He became captain under the management of Ossie Ardiles, and was skipper when Glenn Hoddle led the Wiltshire club into the Premiership.

But as soon as they were promoted Swindon sold Calderwood to Spurs, with Ardiles returning in July 1993 to pay £1.25 million for the defender. He had his ups and downs at first, but once Gerry Francis took over he became a regular in the Spurs defence and made his Scotland debut a few months later in March 1995.

Good in the air and useful on the ground, Colin Calderwood is a mainstay of Scotland's defence after his footballing rebirth under Gerry Francis

He was ever–present in the heart of the Scotland defence that conceded just two goals in 16 games during 1996 and 1997, scored by Alan Shearer and Paul Gascoigne during Euro 96.

Sol **Campbell**

Sulzeer "Sol" Campbell has suddenly emerged as a key figure not only in the heart of the Spurs defence, but also for Glenn Hoddle's new-look England side. A

Sol CAMPBELL

Born:
18 September 1974
Birthplace:
Newham, London
Height:
6ft 2in
Weight:
14st 4lb
Signed For spurs:
23/9/92 from trainee
Spurs debut:
5 December 1992 vs.
Chelsea
Career:
Spurs 1992–present
(161 apps., 4 goals)
Honours:
9 England caps
1 England "B" cap,
11 U-21 caps,
9 Youth caps
European Youth
Championship winner
in 1993

versatile performer who has turned out at full-back, centre-back, in midfield and attack for Spurs, he is now firmly established as the best young defender in Britain and a first choice at the heart of the England defence.

His growing maturity in a position that usually brings improvement with age was shown in the summer of 1997, when he was outstanding in England's World Cup qualifier in Poland and the Le Tournoi friendly tournament in France.

He especially shone in the latter against Brazil with a combination of athleticism and coolness that nullified the threat of Ronaldo, the world's most expensive player, and brought comparisons with the late, great Bobby Moore.

The good news for Tottenham supporters was that Campbell had just signed a new five-year deal after being the only ever-present player during an injury-ravaged 1996–97 season. He was the supporters' unanimous choice as Player of the Year after confirming the promise he had shown the previous season.

Surprisingly, Sol was a late starter in football, not playing the game seriously until he was 14. He trained with his local side, West Ham, but left after a short period to join Spurs, and progressed to the FA's national School of Excellence at Lilleshall.

His first Spurs appearance was as a 17-year-old

A phenomenal athlete and versatile footballer, Sol Campbell has developed in a very short space of time into the best young defender in Britain

substitute striker when he scored in a 2–1 defeat by Chelsea in 1992. The following season he became a regular in defence, having helped England win the European Youth Championship in 1993. He alternated between full-back and central defence, but finally settled in as a central defender when Gerry Francis took over from Ossie Ardiles, and is now determined to stick to that position.

Campbell's England debut was as a substitute against Hungary shortly before Euro '96, where he made one appearance, also as substitute, against Scotland. His full debut came in the World Cup qualifier in Georgia a few months later, and he has grown in stature with every game since then. He is now a regular in former Spurs' star Glen Hoddle's England squad.

He has every attribute essential to the modern defender – pace, power, positional sense and calmness under pressure. He is not afraid to bring the ball out of defence and run at players and, if he can improve his long passing, could become the complete defender. Sol is already being tipped as a likely future captain of England.

Gordon **Durie**

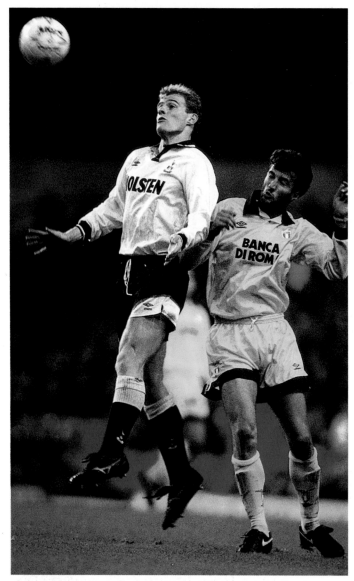

A record signing when bought from Chelsea for £2.2 million, Gordon Durie was another player who failed to live up to his reputation at Spurs

Gordon "Jukebox" Durie proved such a hit in Scottish football that Chelsea paid £400,000 to acquire his talents from Hibernian in 1986, and Spurs paid a then club record £2.2 million to sign him five years later.

Yet Durie never quite lived up to his reputation in English football and only started scoring freely again when he returned to Scottish football, after Ossie Ardiles sold him to Rangers following a well-publicized spat in 1993. Durie was a promising young striker in Scotland when Chelsea snapped him up in 1986, and he helped them win the second division championship three years later.

He was never an outstanding goalscorer but worked well alongside Kerry Dixon at Stamford Bridge, and Terry Venables paid a club record £2.2 million to sign him in 1991 to play alongside Gary Lineker.

But the goals did not flow and he scored just 17 times in 78 games, before falling out with Ardiles after a petulant outburst when substituted during a Coca-Cola Cup win over Burnley.

He refused to apologize for his profane display, asked for a transfer and was despatched back to Scotland, where he rediscovered the art of putting the ball in the back of the net and had great success at Glasgow Rangers.

Gordon DURIE

Born:
6 December 1965
Birthplace:
Paisley
Height:
6ft
Weight:
12st
Signed For Spurs:
08/91 for £2.2 million
Spurs debut:
17 August 1991 vs. Southampton
Career:
East Fife 1981–84;
Hibernian 1984–86;
Chelsea 1986–91;
Spurs 1991–93 (78 apps., 17 goals);
Glasgow Rangers 1993–present
Honours:
32 Scotland caps,
1 "B" cap, 4 U-21 caps, Division Two Championship 1989, Scottish Championship 5 times, Scottish Cup 1993, 1996.

Les **Ferdinand**

Les FERDINAND

Born:
8 December 1966
Birthplace:
Acton
Height:
5ft 11in
Weight:
13st 7lbs
Signed For Spurs:
28/07/97 for £6 million
Spurs debut:
10 August 1997 vs. Manchester United
Career:
QPR 1987–95: loans to Brentford 1988 and Besiktas (Tur) 1989 Newcastle 1995–97, Spurs 1997
Honours:
13 England caps

Gerry Francis paid a new club record of £6 million to sign Les Ferdinand from Newcastle in July 1997, linking up with the England striker for the second time.

It was Francis who helped Ferdinand develop from a reserve striker at QPR into an international, making his England debut in 1993. Ferdinand started as a part-time player with non-League side Southall and then Hayes before joining QPR in 1987, teaming up with Francis three years later. By the time Newcastle paid a club

Gerry Francis turned Les Ferdinand into a world-class striker at QPR and is hoping the former Newcastle man can bring silverware to Spurs

February 1994; but though a fans' favourite, Fox suffered most when Andy Cole was sold to Manchester United, not least because the deal took right-winger Keith Gillespie to St James Park, and he was lured to Spurs for £4.2 million in October 1995, at once winning over the fans with a superb display in the 2–1 win over Arsenal a few weeks later. But when Gerry Francis switched systems, using three central defenders and two wing-backs rather than wingers, Fox was out in the cold again.

A trickster who can cross superbly and score goals himself Fox brings a touch of magic to White Hart Lane when on song.

Ruel FOX	
Born:	14 January 1968
Birthplace:	Ipswich
Height:	5ft 6in
Weight:	10st 5lb
Signed For Spurs:	6/10/95 for £4.2 million
Spurs debut:	14 October 1995 vs. Nottingham Forest
Career:	Norwich City 1986–94; Newcastle United 1994–95; Spurs 1995–present (60 apps., 7 goals)
Honours:	2 England "B" caps

record £6 million for him in 1995 he was firmly established as one of the top strikers in Europe. When Newcastle decided to sell him in 1997 after two highly successful years in the North-East, Ferdinand immediately chose Spurs, the club he supported as a boy. Strong, quick and superb in the air, Ferdinand is the complete striker and has proved his worth for his country many times.

Ruel **Fox**

Ruel Fox reversed a trend when he signed to Spurs from Newcastle in October 1995. For years Norwich had been signing ex-Spurs players: now Spurs had a winger who learned his trade at Carrow Road.

Ipswich-born Fox was perhaps the brightest of the stars who propelled Norwich to the top three of the Premiership and a famous UEFA Cup run in 1993. That earned him a £2.5 million move to Newcastle in

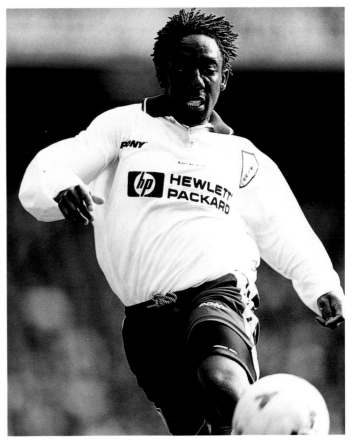

Fast and tricky on the ball, Ruel Fox is an old-fashioned winger who can also weigh in with his fair share of goals

Micky **Hazard**

A skilful and popular midfielder, Micky Hazard brought a touch of the old flair back to Spurs when he returned in the mid-Nineties

Micky Hazard's best years were behind him when he rejoined Spurs in the Premiership in 1993, but he merits a place as a Spurs favourite for his contribution a decade earlier.

Although born in Sunderland, Hazard joined Tottenham as a schoolboy in 1975. He made his debut in the 1979–80 season, and spent the next five years living in the shadow of Glenn Hoddle and Ossie

Ardiles. Hazard did not play a full season for Spurs in that time, but he picked up winners' medals in the FA Cup in 1982 and UEFA Cup two years later.

He had great skill, vision and distribution but could not survive under the shadow of Hoddle, and left for Chelsea in September 1985 for £310,000. His delightful touch made him a crowd favourite at Chelsea, but his maverick style led to a brief spell at Portsmouth before he teamed up again with Ardiles at Swindon Town.

When Hoddle took over at Swindon, Hazard was still the creative midfield force and helped them win promotion to the top flight for the first time in 1992. Having achieved this, he jumped at the chance of a return to White Hart Lane under Ardiles in November 1993 for a bargain £50,000.

A serious back injury meant that he played only two half-seasons, but he still produced flashes of the magic that had endeared him to Spurs fans a decade earlier.

Micky HAZARD

Born:
5 February 1960
Birthplace:
Sunderland
Height:
5ft 8in
Weight:
11st 8lb
Signed For Spurs:
2/02/78 from apprentice and 3/11/93 for £50,000
Spurs debut:
19 April 1980 vs. Everton
Career:
Spurs 1978–85 (139 app. 23 goals); Chelsea 1985–90; Portsmouth 1990; Swindon Town 1990–93; Spurs 1993–95 (31 apps., 2 goals)
Honours:
FA Cup Winner 1982, UEFA Cup Winner 1984

David **Howells**

Spurs' second-longest-serving player after Gary Mabbutt, David Howells is the unsung hero and midfield anchor man of the side.

Having trained with the club since his schooldays, the Guildford-born player signed YTS forms in 1984 and made his debut in 1986, scoring the winning goal in a 2–1 victory at Sheffield Wednesday.

At the time he was an England youth striker, and although Terry Venables once described him as the best finisher at the club, he has long since settled into a central midfield role. He played an important part in the 1991 FA Cup triumph, both in the semi-final against Arsenal and the final win over Nottingham Forest.

A serious knee injury threatened his career in 1993,

David HOWELLS

Born:
15 December 1967
Birthplace:
Guildford
Height:
6ft
Weight:
12st 7lb
Signed For Spurs:
28 January 1985 from trainee
Spurs debut:
22 February 1986 vs. Sheffield Wednesday
Career:
Spurs 1985–present (314 apps., 27 goals)
Honours:
2 England U-19, 8 Youth caps, FA Cup winner 1991

but he fought back to prove his effectiveness and has become a key player in Gerry Francis's teams.

He missed only four games at the end of 1996–97, his testimonial season, and one in which he was called upon as captain when both Gary Mabbutt and Teddy Sheringham were absent.

Strong in the tackle, good in the air and tactically astute, he is a great example of the modern midfielder and many people judge him unlucky never to have received recognition at England level.

After ten years at Spurs, the often-underrated David Howells finally found his niche as a ball-winning midfield anchorman under Gerry Francis

Gary **Mabbutt**

Club captain Gary Mabbutt has just completed 15 years at Tottenham and is still one of the bravest and most consistent defenders in the Premiership. Such bravery, however, has cost him dear, with a string of serious injuries that might have finished lesser players. Only 18 minutes into the 1996–97 season he broke his left leg so badly at Blackburn Rovers that he was ruled out for the season. Mabbutt underwent three operations and spent most of the year in rehabilitation regaining his fitness, a battle not many 35-year-olds would have won.

Yet Mabbutt is no stranger to overcoming adversity. As a diabetes sufferer, doctors advised him against a career in professional football, but his never-say-die attitude has helped him overcome the illness.

The son of former Bristol Rovers star Ray Mabbutt, Gary followed in his father's footsteps to play for his hometown club. He won England Youth and Under-21 honours before writing to every first-division club asking for a trial. Bill Nicholson, then in charge of scouting, invited him to White Hart Lane and he was signed for a bargain £105,000 in August 1982.

Mabbutt made his Spurs debut in the 1982 Charity Shield, and was back at Wembley a few months later to play at right-back for England against West Germany, the first of his 16 full caps.

His versatility meant that he could play in defence, midfield or even up front occasionally, and he was a valuable member of the triumphant 1984 UEFA Cup-winning squad.

In 1986 David Pleat switched him to centre-back alongside Richard Gough, who he replaced as captain the following year. By then he'd had the misfortune of scoring Coventry's winner in the 1987 FA Cup final with an own-goal, having earlier put Spurs ahead. But he

Gary MABBUTT

Born:
23 August 1961
Birthplace:
Bristol
Height:
5ft 10in
Weight:
13st 1lb
Signed For Spurs:
11/08/82 for £105,000
Spurs debut:
21 August 1982 vs. Liverpool (FA Charity Shield)
Career:
Bristol Rovers 1979–1982; Spurs 1982–present (607 apps., 38 goals)
Honours:
16 England caps, 9 "B" caps, 6 U-21 caps, 11 Youth caps, UEFA Cup winner 1984, FA Cup winner 1991 MBE

Gary Mabbutt has overcome major setbacks to become one of the game's most respected players

was back four years later to lift the cup when Spurs beat Forest 2–1, a moment he described as the proudest of his career.

Mabbutt was awarded the MBE for services to football in 1994, ironically while recovering from horrific facial injuries he received from the elbow of John Fashanu during a league match against Wimbledon.

His astute positional sense, decisive tackling and commanding presence have made him one of the outstanding defenders of his era, and as a leading member of the PFA he is widely regarded as a model professional both on and off the pitch.

Vinny **Samways**

Vinny Samways was the "nearly" man of Tottenham during the late 1980s and early '90s.

Brought through the youth ranks in the tradition of Glenn Hoddle and Micky Hazard, Samways was a skilful, ball-playing midfielder who never quite made his mark.

Hoddle and Ardiles were always going to be a dif-

ficult act to follow, but Samways was unfortunate to come into a team which struggled to support his silky skills.

He suffered abuse from the crowd but won them over with his superb performances in the 1991 FA Cup run, particularly in the semi-final against Arsenal.

One failing was that he did not score enough goals for a player of his undoubted ability, and he eventually left to join Everton in August 1994 for £2.2 million. But he failed to fit into the muscular regime at Goodison Park and moved on to Spanish football in 1996.

Vinny SAMWAYS

Born:
27 October 1968
Birthplace:
Bethnal Green, London
Height:
5ft 8in
Weight:
11st
Signed For Spurs:
9/11/85 from apprentice
Spurs debut:
2 May 1987 vs. Nottingham Forest
Career:
Spurs 1987–94 (247 apps., 17goals); Everton 1994–96 (loans to Wolves and Birmingham), Las Palmas 1996–present
Honours:
5 England U-21 caps, 8 Youth caps, FA Cup-winner 1991

Another player who never quite fulfilled his potential, Vinny Samways emerged as a skilful but erratic midfielder before leaving for Everton

John SCALES	
Born:	4 July 1966
Birthplace:	Harrogate
Height:	6ft 2in
Weight:	13st 5lb
Signed For Spurs:	8/12/96 for £2.6 million
Spurs debut:	21 December 1996 vs Sheffield Wednesday
Career:	Leeds United 1983–85 Bristol Rovers 1985–87 Wimbledon 1987–94 Liverpool 1994–96 Spurs 1996–present (12 apps., 0 goals)
Honours:	3 England caps, 2 "B" caps, FA Cup winner 1988, Coca-Cola Cup-winner 1995.

John **Scales**

John Scales was another player who took the long route to joining up with Spurs – or at least with manager Gerry Francis. The stylish defender was signed from Liverpool in December 1996 for £3.5 million after he turned down a move back to his first club, Leeds United, who had released him as a youngster in 1985.

Instead, Scales started his league career with Bristol Rovers as a team-mate of Gerry Francis, who was coming to the end of his playing days. When Francis returned to Rovers after coaching at Wimbledon in 1987, he found that Scales had just made the opposite journey after being signed by Bobby Gould for £70,000.

Scales appeared as substitute for Wimbledon in their famous FA Cup Final triumph over Liverpool in 1988 and went on to become one of the best central defenders in the Premiership.

Eventually Liverpool paid £3.5 million for him in 1994, and Scales featured at the heart of their defence for their 1995 Coca-Cola Cup victory and 1996 FA Cup Final defeat.

After joining Spurs six months later, he immediately added composure and stability at the back as one of those rare defenders who appears completely comfortable on the ball.

He played for England in the Umbro Cup against Brazil, Sweden and Japan in 1995 and was a member of the squad that travelled to France for Le Tournoi in June 1997.

John Scales added vast experience to Spurs' defence when he was signed from Liverpool

Steve Sedgley

Steve SEDGLEY

Born:
26 May 1968
Birthplace:
Enfield
Height:
6ft 1in
Weight:
13st 13lb
Signed For Spurs:
28 July 1989 for
£750,000
Spurs debut:
19 August 1989 vs.
Luton Town
Career:
Coventry City 1986–89
Spurs 1989–94
(211 apps., 11 goals)
Ipswich Town
1994–present
Honours:
112 England U-21 caps
FA Cup-winner 1991

Steve Sedgley was another local boy who, like Teddy Sheringham, served his apprenticeship elsewhere before coming to play for Tottenham.

Enfield-born Sedgley played for Spurs in their 1983 South East Counties youth team but it was Coventry City with whom he turned professional in June 1986, and he was on the substitute's bench when they beat Spurs in the 1987 FA Cup final.

Two years later he moved back to Spurs for £750,000, having won England Under-21 honours. Initially a midfielder, Sedgley had most success for Spurs as a central defender and played in that position alongside Gary Mabbutt during the 1991 FA Cup final win over Nottingham Forest.

After five seasons at White Hart Lane, he eventually moved to Ipswich in 1994 for £1 million and became club captain at Portman Road.

A versatile and wholehearted player, Steve Sedgley played in a number of positions during his five years at Spurs

Teddy Sheringham

Despite leaving for Manchester United in a £3.5 million deal in June 1997, Teddy Sheringham will remain a Spurs star. He has been Tottenham's leading scorer during the Premiership years and at the same time proved himself one of the best strikers in Britain. He emerged as first-choice partner for Alan Shearer for England since Euro '96 and is considered as valuable for his support play as his goals.

Sheringham grew up in North London supporting Tottenham but started his career south of the river at Millwall. He had periods learning his trade on loan in Sweden and at Aldershot before forging a prolific partnership with Tony Cascarino to help Millwall win promotion to the first division for the first time in their history in 1987–88.

After scoring a club record of 42 goals in the 1990–91 season, Sheringham was sold to Nottingham Forest for £2 million – another club record. Early the following season, Terry Venables signed him for £2.1 million to replace Gary Lineker, who had left for Japan, and after a slow start he finished the season as the Premiership's top scorer with 22 League goals.

A serious knee injury kept him out for most of the following season as Spurs hovered above the relegation zone, but he still scored an impressive 15 goals in 21 games.

Sheringham really blossomed into an international striker when he teamed up with Jürgen Klinsmann in 1994–95, the pair scoring 52 goals between them. When Klinsmann left Spurs the next season Sheringham forged an understanding with new signing Chris Armstrong, forming a 46-goal partnership, but with one or both players out through injury for much of the 1996–97 season, Tottenham struggled to score goals.

Sheringham's international career was a long time coming. He had an

Teddy SHERINGHAM

Born:
2 April 1966
Birthplace:
Highams Park, London
Height:
6ft
Weight:
12st 8lb
Signed For Spurs:
28/08/92 for
£2.1 million
Spurs debut:
30 August 1992 vs.
Ipswich Town
Career:
Millwall 1983–91
Aldershot 1985 (loan)
Nottingham Forest
1991–92
Spurs 1992–1997
(197 apps., 98 goals)
Honours:
28 England caps
1 U-21 cap
11 Youth caps

unhappy debut under Graham Taylor in Poland in 1993, but began to establish himself as a regular in the England side shortly before the 1996 European Championship. He played in all five England games during Euro '96, scoring twice and being voted man of the match in the 4–1 mauling of Holland.

An intelligent and creative player, Sheringham is adept at dropping deep to draw out defenders before timing his runs into the attack with perfection. He is a superb header of the ball, can score with both feet and has recently added the ability to score from long range with free-kicks. He had the honour of captaining Tottenham for most of the 1996–97 season because of Gary Mabbutt's absence through injury. His vision and ability will be missed at Spurs.

Andy Sinton

A hardworking and goalscoring winger, Andy Sinton enjoyed a new lease of life when he moved to Spurs in 1996 after three slow years

Andy Sinton was a very long time coming to Tottenham, finally signing in February 1996 after having had trials with the club as a youngster 15 years earlier!

Spurs were one of the clubs chasing Newcastle-born Sinton when he was starring for England Schoolboys, but instead he chose unfashionable Cambridge United where he expected to get a first-team chance sooner.

And he was right, playing for the first team at just 17 years old and starring in a struggling side which set a record of 31 consecutive games without a win.

Sinton soon found himself at Brentford, where his game progressed under the guidance of former Spurs captain Steve Perryman, and a move to the big time became inevitable.

QPR paid £350,000 to take him to Loftus Road in March 1989, and he soon found himself under the tutelage of Gerry Francis.

Sinton was a key member of a successful QPR side, providing the ammunition for Les Ferdinand from the wing, and he also won 12 England caps under Graham Taylor.

By August 1993, bigger clubs were after him and he turned down Liverpool and Arsenal to join Sheffield Wednesday for £2.75 million. Injuries and changes of manager affected him badly at Hillsborough, however, and Sinton jumped at the chance to link up with Francis again when Spurs offered £1.5 million for him in January 1996.

The remainder of that season was a stop-start affair because he was cup-tied and then injured, but he returned to his best form in 1996–97 and was close to an England recall.

Hard-working, honest and a great crosser of the ball, Andy Sinton is finally enjoying his football after three years in the wilderness and could prove a great asset to Spurs.

Andy SINTON

Born:
19 March 1966

Birthplace:
Newcastle

Height:
5ft 8in

Weight:
11st 1lb

Signed For Spurs:
23/01/96 for £1.5 m

Spurs debut:
3 February 1996 vs. Liverpool

Career:
Cambridge United 1982–85;
Brentford 1985–89;
QPR 1989–93;
Sheffield Wednesday 1993–96;
Spurs 1996–present (45 apps., 6 goals)

Honours:
12 England caps,
3 "B" caps,
9 Schoolboy caps

Ian WALKER

Born:
31 October 1971
Birthplace:
Watford
Height:
6ft 2in
Weight:
13st 1lb
Signed For Spurs:
4/12/89 from trainee
Spurs debut:
10 April 1991 vs.
Norwich City
Career:
Oxford United 1990
(loan);
Spurs 1991–present
(193 apps.)
Honours:
3 England caps,
9 U-21 caps,
5 U-19 caps,
12 Youth caps,
FA Youth Cup-winner
1990

Ian Walker had trouble last season but is still one of Britain's best 'keepers

Ian Walker

Widely – and unfairly – criticized for allowing Gianfranco Zola to score Italy's winning goal in their World Cup qualifier against England in February 1997, Ian Walker showed his strength of character by defying injury to bounce back to his best form at the end of a difficult season.

Walker admitted that the criticism he received after the Italy game, his full international debut, was his first major setback after a relentless rise to the top. But being both intelligent and down-to-earth, he took it in his stride as part of the learning process. He has had some of the best teachers in the business, after all. His father Mike was a Welsh Under-23 keeper during a long career with Watford and Colchester before becoming a successful manager at Norwich.

After attending the FA's national School of Excellence at Lilleshall, where he worked with leading coach Mike Kelly, Walker signed for Spurs and came under the tutelage of Ray Clemence, then reserve team manager. Since then he has worked with goalkeeping coach Pat Jennings, whose style he emulated in one of his first games by catching a cross one-handed, a move that immediately endeared him to the Spurs fans.

After helping Spurs win the FA Youth Cup in 1990, he made his full debut in 1991, ironically against his father's team Norwich, having had brief loan spells at Oxford and Ipswich. The following season he became a regular in place of the injured Erik Thorstvedt and gradually ousted the Norwegian international from the first team over the next two seasons

He was firmly established as the club's Number One goalkeeper when Gerry Francis arrived in November 1994, and did not miss a game for the next two and a half years until injury forced him out of the last match of the 1996–97 season.

He was first called up to the England set-up in February 1995 and made his debut as a substitute against Hungary the following year, making the final squad for Euro '96. The World Cup qualifier against Italy was his full debut, but nagging shoulder and foot injuries forced him out of subsequent England squads.

A brilliant shot-stopper with quick reflexes, he has the agility and temperament to reach the very top. He is still young in goalkeeping terms and could yet join Ted Ditchburn, Ray Clemence and Pat Jennings in the pantheon of great Spurs keepers.

The Premiership Managers

The hot seat at White Hart Lane has seen its share of success and failure, and the Premiership years have been no different

BEING manager of Tottenham Hotspur is still one of the biggest jobs in British football – and one of the hardest. Such is the tradition of the club, especially since the 1950s, that the fans do not just demand success – they want it delivered in style. It is not enough for a Spurs side to bring back silverware to White Hart Lane if they have to sacrifice the stylish, attacking football style that has been the club's trademark ever since Arthur Rowe's side won the second- and first-division championships in breathtaking style shortly after the war.

Tottenham's fans demand flair, style and most of all, an entertaining side. In modern football it is not easy to be entertaining and win consistently. The enormous amounts of money at stake, and the ever-increasing demand for success, have led to a win-at-all-costs mentality in many quarters.

But Spurs have always had a commitment to entertain. Successive managers have tried, with varying degrees of success, to emulate the style of Rowe and Bill Nicholson, the greatest of all Spurs managers. Their philosophy was perfectly summed up by Danny Blanchflower, captain of the Double-winning side and one of the game's foremost thinkers, when he said:

"Football is not really about winning, or goals, or saves, or supporters...it's about glory. It's about doing things in style, doing them with a flourish; it's about going out to beat the other lot, not waiting for them to die of boredom. It's about dreaming of the glory that the Double brought".

That quote, which has hung in the offices of managers down the years, has been a mixed blessing. For some, the burden of trying to live up to that legacy has led to a fatally naïve approach to attacking football. But for others it has provided the inspiration and guidance to create teams capable of quite breathtaking football.

Tottenham's first official manager was Frank Brettell, who reigned for less than a year from 1898 to 1899. He was followed by John Cameron, the Scottish player-manager who led Spurs to their first FA Cup triumph in 1901. An experienced player with Everton and Scotland, he helped Spurs win the Southern League as well as the Cup; but when he resigned in 1907 his replacement Fred Kirkham was a former referee with no playing or managerial experience. Not surprisingly, he lasted barely a year.

The second successful Spurs manager was Peter McWilliam, a Scot with a similar background to Cameron. His distinguished playing career including winning the FA Cup and three championship medals with Newcastle, and after Spurs were relegated shortly after he took over in 1912, he led them back into the first division and won the FA Cup in 1921. After making way for Billy Minter in 1927, he eventually returned for one more season before the Second World War broke out.

Percy Smith took over from Minter in 1930 with no great success, and former West Ham player Jack Tresadern fared no better during his three years in the hot seat from 1935–38.

After the war, former Arsenal winger Joe Hulme was in charge for three years before Arthur Rowe took over in 1949. Rowe was a Spurs man through and through. Born locally, he played for the club throughout the 1930s and won one England cap, but injury eventually forced him to retire shortly before the war. Always interested in analysing games, he moved to Hungary to see how the game was played on the Continent. He was set to become national coach there but the war intervened and he returned to England, continuing to develop his coaching skills in the army. When the chance came to take over at Spurs in 1949 he immediately put his ideas into practice. His style of quick passing and movement was revolutionary in England at the time, and hugely effective. Spurs won the second-division title and then their first Championship the following year, playing what became known as "push and run".

Ill-health forced Rowe to give way to Jimmy Anderson in 1955, but his legacy was secure, and Bill Nicholson's reign continued it. Terry Neill took over from Nicholson in 1974, but as a former Arsenal player he never really won the fans over.

Keith Burkinshaw was much more like Nicholson. Another blunt Yorkshireman, he built a team of superb entertainers who won the FA Cup twice and a second UEFA Cup, as well as reaching the League Cup final.

Burkinshaw's assistant Peter Shreeves took over in 1985 and made a good title challenge in his first season.

But he was replaced after two years by David Pleat, who could well have become one of Spurs' most successful managers had he stayed longer than 15 months. In that short time he built an innovative and entertaining side that reached the FA Cup final, the League Cup semi-final and finished third in the League.

When Pleat left in 1987 because of allegations about his private life, Terry Venables was the obvious choice to take over. Recently released by Barcelona, the former Tottenham midfielder brought style, glamour and big names back to White Hart Lane, his two major coups being the signings of Paul Gascoigne and Gary Lineker.

When he joined Alan Sugar in buying out former chairman Irving Scholar, Venables became chief executive and installed Shreeves as manager for just one year before the Premier League started in 1992.

Bill NICHOLSON

Bill Nicholson's reign as Tottenham manager could hardly have got off to a better start than the 10–4 demolition of Everton in his first game, in October 1958. But it would take another three years before he was elevated into the pantheon of the all-time greats.

Nicholson was born in Scarborough but was invited to join Spurs as a 17-year-old. His playing career was interrupted by the war but he made one England appearance – scoring a rare goal within 19 seconds of the start against Portugal in 1951.

It was in management that Nicholson was to leave his mark on the British game. In a 16-year period of heady triumph, he built arguably the finest club side seen in English football as Spurs stormed to the first League and FA Cup Double this century. They followed that with another FA Cup and Britain's first success in Europe, although they narrowly missed out on the title again.

When the Double side broke up, Nicholson rebuilt and won the FA Cup in 1967, the League Cup twice, the UEFA Cup once and reached the final again before losing to Feyenoord. That was effectively Nicholson's swansong. Upset by rioting fans and disenchanted with the way money was starting to take over, he remained for a few more months but eventually resigned in 1974, although he later returned to the club as a consultant and celebrated his 60th anniversary with Spurs before retiring in 1997.

Bill Nicholson: Spurs' greatest influence

Terry Venables and Doug Livermore

Tottenham's first season in the Premiership was marked by a new approach to management. Terry Venables had taken over as chief executive and part-owner of the club a year earlier, and the new board had brought back Peter Shreeves as manager for the second time.

But after finishing a disappointing 15th and going out of Europe in the quarter-finals, Spurs adopted a different approach. Shreeves was replaced by Doug Livermore as first-team coach with Ray Clemence as his assistant, while Venables assumed responsibility for overall football affairs as general manager.

Although Venables had done it all as a manager, winning the Spanish championship and reaching the European Cup final with Barcelona, and winning the FA Cup with Spurs, his approach was mostly hands-off. It was only midway through the season, when the team was starting to struggle, that he returned to training-ground duties and began working directly with players again.

Livermore had been at the club for eight years, initially joining as reserve-team manager under Peter Shreeves in 1984. Venables took over as manager in 1987 and he appointed Livermore his assistant two years later, promoting him to first-team coach in 1992 for one year.

Livermore was born in Liverpool and started his

Doug Livermore spent one season as first-team coach under Terry Venables

---

Doug LIVERMORE

Born:
27 December 1947, in Liverpool
Playing career:
Liverpool 1965–70 (18 League apps)
Norwich City 1970–75 (113 League apps, 4 goals)
Bournemouth (loan)1975 (10 League apps)
Cardiff City 1975–77 (84 League apps, 5 goals)
Chester 1977–78 (71 League apps, 6 goals)
Honours:
Second-division champions 1971–72
League Cup runners-up 1973
Promotion from Division Three 1975–76
Managerial career:
Swansea City (assistant manager) 1980–84
Tottenham Hotspur (assistant manager) 1989–92
Tottenham Hotspur (first-team coach) 1992–93
Liverpool (assistant manager) 1994–present
Wales (assistant manager) 1980–88

---

career as a professional at Anfield in 1965. Never a regular at Liverpool, he moved to Norwich in 1970 and helped them win the second-division championship in 1971–72. The following year saw him reach the League Cup final at Wembley – where Norwich lost to Spurs. After a loan spell at Bournemouth he moved to Cardiff in 1975, helping them win promotion and the Welsh Cup. After a brief spell at Chester City, he returned to Cardiff as coach in 1978. He also coached at Norwich before becoming assistant manager of Swansea City in 1980, and became assistant manager of Wales under Mike England until 1988.

The highlight of his Spurs career was as assistant manager during the 1991 FA Cup win over Nottingham Forest, and he went close to repeating that Wembley appearance two years later when he was in charge, with Spurs losing in a packed Wembly semi-final to Arsenal, by a single goal, scored late in the second half by Arsenal captain Tony Adams.

His Spurs side finished eighth in the League and he won the Manager of the Month award for February, but when Venables was ousted and Ossie Ardiles took over, Clemence was sacked and Livermore reverted to being coach and head scout.

He remained at White Hart Lane until four months before Gerry Francis's new regime came to power in November 1994, when he returned to Liverpool as assistant to manager Roy Evans.

The fans backed Terry Venables' buy-out, but he lasted only a year as chief executive

Terry VENABLES

Born:
6 January 1943, Bethnal Green, London

Playing career:
Chelsea 1959–65 (202 League apps, 26 goals)
Tottenham 1966–69 (115 League apps, 5 goals)
QPR 1969–74 (178 League apps, 19 goals)
Crystal Palace 1974–75 (14 League apps)

Honours:
Second-division runners-up 1962–63
League Cup-winners 1965
FA Cup-winners 1967

International honours:
First player to appear for England at all levels: Schoolboy, Amateur, Youth, Under-23 and Senior (Two full caps)

Managerial career:
Crystal Palace 1976–80
QPR 1980–84
Barcelona 1984–87
Tottenham 1987–93
England (coach) 1994–96
Australia (coach)1996–present

Honours:
Second-division champions 1978/79
FA Cup runners-up 1982
Second-division champions 1982/83
Spanish champions 1984/85
European Cup runners-up 1986
FA Cup-winners 1991

Ossie Ardiles

WHEN Ossie Ardiles became manager of Spurs in June 1993, it was the fulfilment of yet another dream for the Argentinian. Always that little bit cleverer than the average footballer, Ardiles was destined for a career in management and held a long-standing ambition to be manager of Tottenham.

It was ironic that, less than 18 months after achieving his aim, it proved to be the job that ruined his reputation and soured his special relationship with the Spurs supporters.

Ardiles was one of the stars of the World Cup when Keith Burkinshaw signed him along with his fellow-countryman Ricky Villa in 1978. The two of them had just helped Argentina win the cup, but it was Ardiles who caught the eye as a brilliant midfield playmaker. It was little wonder that, as a law student and chess player of some note, he brought an intelligent and artistic approach to the game.

He proved to be a sensation in England, despite a difficult start. He overcame the physical nature of English football to thrill fans around the country. His much-publicised dream (even in song) of winning the FA Cup was finally achieved in 1981 in memorable style, with Ricky Villa scoring twice in the final replay victory over Manchester City.

When Britain was put on a war footing with Argentina over the Falkland Islands, Ardiles was diplomatically sent on loan to France's Paris St Germain for six months. He returned to Spurs in 1983 and fought back from a broken leg to gain a UEFA Cup-winners' medal in 1984.

Ardiles eventually left Tottenham in 1988, and had spells at Blackburn, QPR and in the USA before going into management with Swindon Town in 1989.

He transformed Swindon from a long-ball team to a stylish, passing side and they won promotion to the first division before being relegated immediately because of financial irregularities from a previous era.

In March 1991 he was appointed manager of Newcastle, but despite building an attractive side with some promising youngsters soon found himself in the relegation zone and was sacked the following February. He moved to West Bromwich Albion three months later, taking them up to the first division in his first season before becoming Spurs' manager in the summer of 1993.

Despite a great start, with wins at Newcastle and Liverpool, Spurs were hit by injuries to key players such as Gary Mabbutt, Teddy Sheringham and Darren Anderton. They were close to the relegation zone until the final few games of the season and finally finished 15th in the Premiership.

That summer, Ardiles spent big and signed three stars from the USA World Cup – Romanians Ilie Dumitrescu and Gica Popescu, and German superstar Jürgen Klinsmann.

Sadly, it was his belief in attacking football that was to prove his downfall. Using five attack-minded players, Spurs were a joy to watch going forward but leaked goals at an alarming rate.

The early-season excitement was replaced by a run of heavy defeats, and Spurs were dumped out of the League Cup after a 3–0 hammering at Notts County. With this humiliation by the first division's bottom club, the writing was on the wall for Ardiles. Fans who had worshipped him as a genius alongside Glenn Hoddle only a decade earlier were calling for his head, and he was sacked at the end of October 1994.

Unrepentant in his belief in attacking football, he moved to Mexico to manage Guadalajara but lasted only a year. Accompanied by his former assistant at Tottenham, Steve Perryman, Ardiles went to Japan's J-League where he finally had the chance to lift some silverware as manager of Shimizu S-Pulse, winners of the Japanese Cup in 1997.

Ossie ARDILES

Born:
3 August 1952, Cordoba, Argentina

Playing career:
Huracan 1974–78
Spurs 1978–88 (238 League apps, 16 goals)
Paris St Germain 1982–83 on loan (14 apps, 1 goal)
Blackburn Rovers (loan) 1987–88 (5 League apps, 1 goal)
QPR 1988–89 (8 League apps)

Honours:
FA Cup 1981
UEFA Cup 1984

International honours:
World Cup winner with Argentina 1978; 43 caps

Managerial career:
Swindon Town 1989–91
Newcastle United 1991–92
West Bromwich Albion 1992–93
Spurs 1993–94
Guadalajara 1994–1995
Shimizu S-Pulse 1995–present

Managerial honours:
Promotion to Premiership 1989–90
Promotion to Premiership 1992–93
Japanese Cup 1997

Keith Burkinshaw (left) signed Ossie Ardiles as a player, while chairman Alan Sugar (right) brought him back as manager in 1993

Ossie Ardiles was a hero as a player at Spurs but not successful in a 17-month spell in charge

Gerry Francis

GERRY FRANCIS was seen as the saviour of Spurs when he took over from Ossie Ardiles in November 1994. Ossie's dream of a five-man attack taking the Premiership by storm had quickly turned into a nightmare. With Spurs docked six points by the FA over irregular payments from a previous administration, the club was deep in relegation trouble. Spurs were leaking goals like a holed ship lets in water and survival was looking a remote possibility.

Francis changed things so quickly that within five months Spurs were chasing a place in Europe and looking like a certainty for the FA Cup. Although he was regarded largely as a QPR man because of his time as both player and manager at Loftus Road, Gerry Francis had grown up supporting Spurs in the early 1960s.

But it was in his native West London that he made his name as a skilful and powerful midfielder with QPR, scoring goals and showing the sort of shrewdness and leadership qualities that led to him being appointed captain of England at only 23.

Francis was dogged by injury, however, and a particularly bad back problem when he was in his prime kept him out of action for almost two years. He was never the same player again, and finished his career with brief stints around the country, often in the lower leagues.

He was encouraged to move into coaching at Crystal Palace under Terry Venables, before moving on to Coventry as a player in 1982. His first managerial appointment was as player-manager of Exeter City in 1983, but they were relegated that season and he left within a year.

But he learned from the experience, and when he took over at Bristol Rovers in 1987 he took them to the third-division title and a runners'-up spot at Wembley in the Leyland DAF Cup. He also won the third division Manager of the Year award, having worked wonders with slender resources.

His eye for talent and his ability to bring out the best in his players led to a growing reputation, and it was no surprise that QPR brought him back to London as manager in 1991. There he showed his qualities as a coach by helping players such as Les Ferdinand and Andy Sinton develop from modest roots to international football, and he kept the side in the top six on modest resources year after year.

When he walked out of QPR after a row with chairman Richard Thompson, Tottenham immediately approached him to succeed Ardiles. Francis's first game in charge was remarkable. After 45 minutes, Spurs were 3–0 down at home to Aston Villa before they clawed themselves back level, only to lose in the last minute. Even more startling was the transformation of the team's fortunes. Using essentially the same players as Ardiles, Francis took Spurs on an unbeaten run of 11 games including a club record-equalling run of six successive clean sheets. Ultimately the season ended in disappointment with a 4–1 defeat in the FA Cup semi-final against Everton at Elland Road and a final League placing of seventh, just missing out on a European place.

There was also disappointment with the departure of Klinsmann, Popescu and Nick Barmby, with Dumitrescu to leave later. But Francis signed Chris Armstrong for a club record £4.5 million and saw him link up well with Teddy Sheringham. Francis also added wingers Ruel Fox from Newcastle and his former protegé Andy Sinton from Sheffield Wednesday, but with Anderton missing for most of the campaign Spurs again missed out on Europe on the final day of the season.

Midway through the injury-wrecked 1996–97 season he signed reinforcements in the forms of John Scales, Steffen Iversen and Ramon Vega, but by this stage

Gerry FRANCIS

Born:
6 December 1951, Chiswick, London.
Playing career:
QPR 1969–79 (293 League apps, 53 goals)
Crystal Palace 1979–81 (59 League apps, 7 goals)
QPR 1981–82 (17 League apps, 4 goals)
Coventry City 1982–83 (50 League apps, 2 goals)
Exeter City 1983–84 (28 League apps, 3 goals)
Cardiff City (7 League apps, 2 goals)
Swansea City (3 League apps)
Portsmouth (3 League apps)
Bristol Rovers 1985–87 (33 League apps)
Honours:
Second-division runners-up 1972–73
First-division runners-up 1975–76
International honours:
England, 12 caps (8 as captain), 3 goals.
Managerial career:
Exeter City (player-manager) 1983–84.
Bristol Rovers 1987–91.
QPR 1991–94
Tottenham Hotspur 1994–present
Honours:
Third-division champions 1990
Leyland DAF Cup runners-up 1990
Third-division Manager of the Year 1990

Gerry Francis was the obvious choice to replace Ossie Ardiles, and transformed Spurs' fortunes

Tottenham's season was effectively over. Humiliated by a 6–1 League Cup defeat at first-division Bolton, and dumped out of the FA Cup by Manchester United in the third round, Spurs had only a place in Europe left to play for, and that last hope was dead long before the end of the season.

A further blow was the loss of Sheringham at the end of the season, but Francis was able to sign Les Ferdinand, David Ginola and José Dominguez for a total of almost £10 million to strengthen his squad.

Tottenham Managers' Records 1992–97

Doug Livermore 1992–93

	P	W	D	L	For	Ag	Position
FA Premier League:	42	16	11	15	60	66	8th
League home record	21	11	5	5	40	25.	
League away record	21	5	6	10	20	41	
Coca-Cola Cup	4	3		1	8	5	reached fourth round.
FA Cup	5	4		1	4	5	reached semi-finals.
Overall record (League and Cup)	**51**	**23**	**11**	**17**	**82**	**76**	

Ossie Ardiles 1993–94

	P	W	D	L	For	Ag	Position
FA Premiership	42	11	12	19	54	59	15th.
League home record	21	4	8	9	29	33.	
League away record:		7	4	10	25	26.	
Coca-Cola Cup	5	3	1	1	6	3	reached fifth round
FA Cup (* includes win on penalties vs. Peterborough)	3		2*	1	2	5	reached fourth round
Overall record	**50**	**14**	**15**	**21**	**62**	**67**	

Ossie Ardiles 1994–95

	P	W	D	L	For	Ag	Position
FA Premiership	12	4	2	6	21	24	
League home record	6	2	1	3	8	10	
League away record	6	2	1	3	13	14	
Coca-Cola Cup	3	1		2			reached third round
Overall record							
Premiership:	54	15	14	25	75	83	
League home record:	27	6	9	15	37	43	
League away record:	27	9	5	13	38	40	
Overall record (League and Cup):	65	19	17	29	91	100	

Steve Perryman 1994–95 (caretaker manager)

In charge for one game after Ardiles's departure — 0–2 defeat at Blackburn, Nov 1994.

Gerry Francis 1994–95

	P	W	D	L	For	Ag	Position
Premiership:	29	12	12	5	45	32	7th
League home record:	15	8	4	3	24	15	
League away record:	14	4	8	2	21	7	
FA Cup:	6	4	1	1	17	9	reached semi-finals

Gerry Francis 1995–96

	P	W	D	L	For	Ag	Position
Premiership:	38	16	13	9	50	38	
Position: 8th.							
League home record:	19	9	5	5	26	19.	
League away record:	19	7	8	4	24	19	
Coca-Cola Cup:	3	2	1	9	4		reached third round
FA Cup (*includes penalty defeat by Nottingham Forest after 1–1 draw)	5	2	3*		12	6	reached fifth round

Gerry Francis 1996–97

	P	W	D	L	For	Ag	Position
Premiership:	38	13	7	18	44	51	
Position: 10th.							
League home record:	19	8	4	7	19	17	
League away record:	19	5	3	11	25	34	
Coca-Cola Cup:	4	2	1	1	7	8	reached fourth round
FA Cup:	1		1		0	2	reached third round
Overall record (to end of 96/97 season)							
Premiership:	105	41	32	32	139	121	
League home record:	53	25	13	21	69	51	
League away record:	52	16	19	11	70	70	
Overall record (League and Cup):	124	51	37	36	184	150	

Chapter 7

Tottenham's Foreign Stars

From Ardiles to Ginola, foreign players have held a special fascination for Spurs fans. Here are the cream of the Premiership crop

GIVEN the appearances of players such as Ossie Ardiles, Ricky Villa and Jürgen Klinsmann, it should come as no surprise to learn that Tottenham were the first English side to sign a foreign player. But few people realise that the first foreigner – and the first German in English football – arrived almost 90 years earlier than Klinsmann!

Max Seeburg was the first overseas player to appear in the Football League when he played for Tottenham against Hull in September 1908. He only played one more game, a London FA Charity Cup win over QPR, but Spurs had set in motion a trend that was to bring glamour, glory and heartache to White Hart Lane.

Ardiles and Villa were the most sensational signings when Keith Burkinshaw brought the Argentinian World Cup-winners over in 1978. With a few exceptions, English football had been reluctant to embrace overseas footballers up to that point. But the Argentinians changed the whole perspective and opened up the doors for a flood of foreign talent.

It was fitting, then, that Ardiles was manager when Tottenham initiated the next move forward in foreign transfers, 16 years later. The signing of Jürgen Klinsmann, and the German's subsequent success in England, proved to be the catalyst for a host of established world-class superstars to try their luck in the Premiership. Previous imports, Ardiles excepted, had been good-quality players but not world-class. But Klinsmann's move was quickly followed by an influx of genuine superstars such as Ruud Gullit, Gianluca Vialli, Juninho, Gianfranco Zola and Fabrizio Ravanelli, and earned English football new respect from the rest of the world.

Like most English clubs Spurs have had their fair share of foreign players during the Premiership years, with varying degrees of success. While Klinsmann was a spectacular hit, Romanians Ilie Dumitrescu and Gica Popescu never lived up to their reputations during their brief stay at Tottenham.

Other, less famous, foreigners have proved hugely popular with the fans and invaluable to the club. Nayim, Erik Thorstvedt and Ronny Rosenthal have all served Spurs well, and the new generation of Continental players is represented by Ramon Vega, Steffen Iversen, Allan Nielsen and David Ginola, as well as Jose Dominguez.

Jürgen **Klinsmann**

Spurs fans had to pinch themselves when it was announced that Jürgen Klinsmann was to join the club in August 1994. Chairman Alan Sugar pulled off a massive coup in typically glamorous style when he conducted negotiations from his yacht in the South of France to sign the German striker from Monaco for a bargain price of £2 million.

Here was a genuine world-class player, and the only doubts in the minds of Spurs fans were about Klinsmann's reputation as a "diver" in the penalty box. The supporters need not have worried. He opened his introductory press conference by making a joke of the issue, asking for directions to the nearest diving school, and went on to conduct himself immaculately on the pitch.

Klinsmann marked his debut at Sheffield Wednesday with the winning goal, before he was carried off on a stretcher. He then further endeared himself to the fans with two goals, one a spectacular overhead kick, on his home debut against Everton.

Jürgen Klinsmann's one stunning season at Spurs sparked an influx of world-class stars to England

Klinsmann didn't stop scoring as he went on to enjoy arguably his finest club season, hitting 29 goals in 50 games and re-establishing himself as one of the world's best strikers. He struck up a great partnership with Teddy Sheringham, leading Spurs into the FA Cup semi-finals and within a point of qualifying for a place in Europe in the UEFA Cup.

Klinsmann's profile and career were rejuvenated during his season in England, but when Bayern Munich approached him he decided to return to Germany. It was an acrimonious departure and ultimately turned out to be an unhappy experience for Klinsmann. Although he won the UEFA Cup with Bayern in his first season, scoring a competition record 15 goals, he soon fell out with captain Lothar Matthaus and coach Giovanni Trapattoni. By summer 1997 he was on the move again and, despite speculation that he would return to England with Tottenham, eventually signed for Italian Serie A side Sampdoria.

Having started his career in his native Stuttgart, first with the Kickers and then with the bigger Vfb Stuttgart, Klinsmann moved to Italy when Inter Milan signed him in 1989. At the time he was German Footballer of the Year, and a year later played a key part in helping Germany win the World Cup.

By the time Germany came to defend their trophy, in USA '94 Klinsmann had moved to French side Monaco. But he found it hard to motivate himself in front of the low crowds Monaco attract and jumped at the chance to play in the Premiership.

After leaving Spurs in 1995, he made an emotional return to England a year later when he captained Germany to the European Championship title in 1996. Undoubtedly a world-class goalscorer, Klinsmann was the perfect professional and, while his stay at Tottenham was all too brief, his professionalism made an indelible mark on the players around him.

Jürgen KLINSMANN

Born: 30 July 1964
Birthplace: Goppingen, Germany
Ht: 6ft 2in
Wt: 12st 13lbs
Signed for Spurs: 3/8/94,
Career:
1981 Stuttgart Kickers,
1984 Vfb Stuttgart,
1989 Inter Milan,
1992 AS Monaco,
1994 Spurs,
1995 Bayern Munich,
1997 Sampdoria.
Spurs record:
50 apps, 29 goals
Honours:
97 German caps,
World Cup-winner 1990,
European Championship winner 1996, UEFA Cup 1991 (Inter) & 1996 (Bayern),
West German Footballer of the Year 1989 and 1994, England Footballer of the Year 1995.

Ilie **Dumitrescu**

Signed for Spurs by Ossie Ardiles after impressing in the 1994 World Cup, where he famously helped Romania to destroy Argentina, Ilie Dumitrescu joined Jürgen Klinsmann as a big-money signing in the summer of 1994.

He had been voted Romania's player of the year a season earlier as a top-scoring attacking midfielder with silky skills and an eye for goal. He showed all of this to great effect against Argentina when he scored twice and set up the third goal for Gheorghe Hagi.

Ardiles signed him from Steaua Bucharest straight after the tournament, breaking Tottenham's transfer record with a £2.6 million fee. Dumitrescu was part of Ardiles' "Famous Five" attacking side, and looked set to be a major player in Premiership football. But, as he admitted himself, he had little idea about tracking

Ilie DUMITRESCU

Born: 6 January 1969
Birthplace: Bucharest, Romania
Ht: 5ft 9in
Wt: 10st 7lbs
Signed for Spurs: 3 August 1994 for £2.6 million
Career:
1986 Steaua Bucharest (Rom)
(loan to FC Olt 1987–88)
1994 Spurs
(loan to Sevilla (Spa) 1995)
1996 West Ham United
1997 FC America (Mexico)
Spurs record:
20 apps, 5 goals
Honours:
55 Romania caps, Romanian League Championship 1989, 1993 and 1994, Romanian Cup-winner 1989 and 1992

back and defending, and was sacrificed a few months later when Gerry Francis took over to steady a shaky side.

He went on loan to Sevilla in Spain but returned at the start of the following season. Still unable to command a regular place, he eventually moved to West Ham for £1.5 million in March 1996 after a protracted attempt to gain a work permit. But he was struck by injuries at West Ham and moved on less than a year later to Mexican side FC America.

Romanian World cup star Ilie Dumitrescu, Spurs' £2.6 million transfer record-breaker

Gheorghe "Gica" **Popescu**

Gica Popescu was Ossie Ardiles's third big-money signing, following Ilie Dumitrescu and Jürgen Klinsmann, when he was bought from PSV Eindhoven in September 1994.

Popescu had been one of the key players in Romania's rise to world prominence in the 1990s, helping them to success in the World Cups of 1990 and 1994. A strong and skilful player, confident in the air and capable on the ground, he could play at sweeper, in defence or as a holding midfielder. Ardiles described him as the perfect all-round player when he signed him, but Popescu strug-

Gheorghe "Gica" POPESCU

Born: 9 October 1967,
Birthplace: Calafat, Romania
Ht: 6ft 2in
Wt: 12st 7lbs
Signed for Spurs: 6 Sept 1994 for £2.9 million
Career:
Universitatea Craiova (Rom)
Steaua Bucharest (Rom)
1990 PSV Eindhoven (Hol)
1994 Spurs
1995 Barcelona (Spa)
1997 Galatasaray (Tur).
Spurs record:
28 apps, 3 goals
Honours:
71 Romania caps, Romanian League 1988, Romanian Cup 1989, Romanian Footballer of the Year 1990, 1991, 1992, 1993, Dutch League Championship 1991, 1992, Spanish Cup and Super Cup 1997, European Cup-winners' Cup 1997.

gled to come to terms with English football. Too often he was bypassed in midfield and he found it hard to cope with the physical nature of the Premiership. But his place in Spurs history was assured when he scored the only goal of the North London derby in January 1995 to sink rivals Arsenal.

Before that season was over, however, he announced his desire to go back to Europe and was sold to Barcelona in May 1995 for £3.1 million. There, ironically, he replaced Ronald Koeman, whose boots he had also stepped into when joining PSV Eindhoven after Italia '90. As captain, he led the Catalan side to the European Cup-winners' Cup and Spanish Cup in 1997 before moving to Turkey with Galatasaray.

Allan **Nielsen**

Allan Nielsen was Tottenham's only signing during summer 1996 when Gerry Francis paid Danish side Brondby £1.65 million for the attacking midfielder. Nielsen joined Bayern Munich in 1989 as a highly-regarded 17-year-old, but could not oust established stars in the first team and returned home to Denmark after playing just one game in three years.

He rediscovered his form at Odense and helped them to European success before moving to FC Copenhagen three years later. Within a year he was at Brondby and helped the Danish team knock Liverpool out of that season's UEFA Cup. Spurs signed him the following summer. He had been part of the Danish side during Euro '96, having established his international credentials in spectacular style.

Nielsen had set a world record in international football when he scored within 60 seconds of his debut for Denmark as a substitute. He was voted Denmark's best player during the 1995–96 season, beating off competition from Brian Laudrup and Peter Schmeichel, but nevertheless took a while to settle into English football but ended his first

season at Spurs with a satisfactory six goals in 33 games.

A strong runner and tackler, Francis compared Nielsen to a young Alan Ball when he signed him. Nielsen's long throws have also added to Tottenham's armoury and he can score with both feet and his head.

Allan NIELSEN

Born: 13 March 1971
Birthplace: Esbjerg, Denmark
Ht: 5ft 8in
Wt: 11st 2lbs
Signed for Spurs: 4 August 1996 for £1.65 million
Career:
Esbjerg (Den)
1989 Bayern Munich (Ger)
1991 Odense (Den)
1994 FC Copenhagen (Den)
1995 Brondby (Den), 1996 Spurs
Spurs record:
33 apps, 6 goals
Honours:
11 Denmark caps

Allan Nielsen developed during the 1996–97 season as an industrious and goalscoring midfielder

Nayim

Nayim arrived at Spurs in 1989 from Barcelona as part of the £1.5 million package that brought Gary Lineker to White Hart Lane and soon established himself as a crowd favourite.

Mohammed Ali Amar, to give him his full name, was born in the Spanish colony of Ceuta in North Africa but his dual Moroccan and Spanish citizenship has allowed him to play at Under-21 level for Spain. He had joined Barcelona as a schoolboy and played under Terry Venables before suffering a serious knee injury which kept him out of action for a year.

When Venables moved to Spurs, he brought Nayim over on loan before signing him in the summer of 1989. An inventive player with great ball skill and a spectacular shot, his greatest goal for Tottenham was a dipping volley from 40 yards against Liverpool in 1991. That was shortly after he had been part of the FA Cup-winning side, having gone on as a substitute when Paul Gascoigne was injured early in the final.

He moved back to Spain for family reasons two years later, joining Real Zaragoza and helping them win the Spanish Cup before going on to win the European Cup-winners' Cup against Arsenal, cementing a place in Spurs history with the goal for which he will always be remembered. His spectacular volley from the half-way line embarrassed England and Arsenal goalkeeper David Seaman as it soared over his head into the net: the winning goal with what was virtually the last kick of the game.

That one goal alone ensured Nayim's name would be chanted by Spurs fans long after he left White Hart Lane.

Nayim: famed for one great goal against Arsenal

NAYIM

Born: 5 November 1966
Birthplace: Ceuta, Morocco
Ht: 5ft 8in
Wt: 11st 4lbs
Signed for Spurs:
28 July 1989 for £300,000
Career:
Barcelona (Spa),
1989 Spurs
1993 Real Zaragoza (Spa)
1997 Logrones (Spa)
Spurs record:
144 apps, 18 goals
Honours:
FA Cup 1991, Spanish Cup 1994, European Cup winners' Cup 1995

Steffen Iversen

Steffen Iversen was hailed as the new Jürgen Klinsmann when he joined Spurs from Rosenborg of Trondheim for £2.6 million in December 1996. Quick, blond and a prolific scorer, the comparisons with Klinsmann were obvious, especially when he inherited the German striker's Number 18 shirt. But the young Norwegian was quick to point out that he was his own man, and soon excited Spurs fans with his powerful and intelligent play alongside Teddy Sheringham in attack.

He had shown those same qualities playing for the Norwegian Under-21 side, where he was a prolific scorer, and with Rosenborg whom he had helped to the quarter-finals of the Champions' League.

Gerry Francis had tracked the 20-year-old Iversen for more than a year and the negotiaing team of Claude Littner and Daniel Sugar had to fight off some of Europe's

Steffen IVERSEN

Born: 10 November 1976,
Birthplace: Oslo, Norway
Ht: 6ft 2in
Wt: 12st 10lbs
Signed for Spurs:
4 December 1996 for
£2.6 million
Career:
Rosenborg (Swe)
1996 Spurs
Spurs record:
16 apps, 6 goals
Honours:
18 Norway Under-21 caps

top clubs to sign him. The young Norwegian went straight into the Spurs first team to replace the injured Chris Armstrong, and showed what he could do when he hit a hat-trick in a 4–0 win at Sunderland.

A knee operation to remove a cyst meant he missed the end of the season but provided him with a much-needed rest after playing without a break for almost two years. Good in the air and able to score with both feet, Iversen is still young and could well emerge as a major force in Premiership and international football.

Gerry Francis headed off some of Europe's top clubs to sign Steffen Iversen from Rosenborg

Ramon **Vega**

Ramon Vega moved to Tottenham in January 1997 just six months after turning them down to join Italian Serie A side Cagliari. The Swiss defender had been wanted by both clubs when he decided to leave Grasshoppers of Zurich after playing a key role for Switzerland in Euro '96.

He chose Cagliari but soon decided he would rather play in England, and Gerry Francis finally got his man midway through the season. Although injuries and suspension limited his appearances, he returned to the side late in the season and immediately showed himself to be a top-quality defender.

Born in Olten, near Zurich, of Spanish parents, Vega did not officially become a Swiss citizen until shortly before making his international debut, in 1993. Tall, strong and comfortable with the ball at his feet, Vega soon established himself as a respected international defender and has captained his country. He has brought European style to the Tottenham side and added to Gerry Francis's options in defence.

> **Ramon VEGA**
>
> **Born:** 14 June 1971
> **Birthplace:** Olten, Switzerland
> **Ht:** 6ft 3in
> **Wt:** 13st
> **Signed for Spurs:**
> 7 January 1997 for £3.75 million
> **Career:**
> Trimbach (Swi), Olten (Swi), Grasshoppers Zurich (Swi), 1996 Cagliari (Ita)
> 1997 Spurs
> **Spurs record:**
> 8 apps, 1 goal
> **Honours:**
> 16 Switzerland caps, Swiss League Championship 1995 and 1996, Swiss Cup-winner 1994

Erik **Thorstvedt**

Erik Thorstvedt was a hugely popular goalkeeper with Spurs and one of the first Norwegians to make a major impact in English football.

"Erik The Viking", as he was immediately and obviously nicknamed, made an inauspicious start when he fumbled a shot from Nigel Clough to hand Nottingham Forest victory on his debut in 1989. But he went on to prove himself a world-class performer and was rewarded with an FA Cup winners' medal in 1991. He won 98 caps for Norway, including appearing at the 1994 World Cup finals.

Goalkeeper Erik "The Viking" Thorstvedt has been a huge hit with fans both at Spurs, where he spent eight years, and in his native Norway

Erik THORSTVEDT

Born: 28 October 1962
Birthplace: Stavanger, Norway
Ht: 6 ft 4in
Wt: 14st 3lbs
Signed for Spurs:
22 Dec 1988 for £400,000
Career:
Eik Tonsberg (Nor), Viking Stavanger (Nor), 1985 Borussia Mönchengladbach (Ger), 1987 IFK Gothenburg (Swe), 1988–1996 Spurs
Spurs record:
218 apps
Honours:
98 Norway caps,
1991 FA Cup-winner

Tall, imposing and a great shot-stopper, he first made his name in his native Stavanger with the Viking club, and was soon signed by Borussia Mönchengladbach. But his spell in Germany was not a happy one and he returned to Scandinavia with IFK Gothenburg of Sweden in 1987. Though he had previously had trials with both Spurs and QPR in 1984, work permit problems blocked any move. Eventually he signed for Spurs in 1988 from Gothenburg. He became a first-team regular until a succession of injuries and the emergence of Ian Walker kept him out of the side.

After retiring because of a serious back problem in July 1996, he returned to Norway and became director of football at Viking.

Ronny **Rosenthal**

True to his explosive nickname of "Rocket", Ronny Rosenthal arrived in England with a bang, scoring seven goals in eight games to help win Liverpool the League Championship in 1990.

The Israeli international striker had been playing in Belgium with Standard Liège before Liverpool signed him for £1 million. His hit-or-miss style and willingness to run at defenders endeared him to fans.

He was unable to command a regular place at Liverpool and Ossie

Ronny ROSENTHAL

Born: 4 October 1963
Birthplace: Haifa, Israel
Ht: 5ft 11in
Wt: 12st 10lbs
Signed for Spurs:
26 January 1994 for £250,000
Career:
Maccabi Haifa (Isr)
FC Bruges (Bel)
Standard Liège (Bel):
loans to Luton and Liverpool
1990 Liverpool, 1994 Spurs
1997 Watford
Spurs record:
100 apps, 11 goals
Honours:
59 Israel caps
Israeli League Championship 1985, Belgian League Championship 1988, Football League Championship 1990

"Rocket" Ronny Rosenthal: a favourite with fans

Ardiles signed him for Spurs in January 1994 for £250,000, initially as cover for the injured Teddy Sheringham. He was used mostly as a wide player at Spurs, and sealed his reputation as a "Super-sub" in an amazing FA Cup tie at Southampton. Spurs were trailing 2–0 in the fifth-round replay when he went on as a substitute and scored a sparkling hat-trick to turn the game around and win 6–2 in extra-time.

That feat alone will ensure his place in the hearts of the Spurs fans. Reaching the end of his contract in 1997, he was given a free transfer, and joined Watford.

David **Ginola**

David Ginola's capture from Newcastle in July 1997 brought a lot of the old swagger back to White Hart Lane. The flamboyant French winger played in the Spurs style, with his tricks on the ball, his vision and his ability to open up a game with a flick or a pass. His flair brought immediate reminders of players such as Waddle, Hoddle and Gascoigne, and he was similarly unlikely to track back in deference to his defensive duties.

Ginola started his career in the south of France as a teenager with Nice, but did not earn a professional contract and instead joined Racing Club of Toulon. He moved to Matra Racing for three years, served one season at Brest and then hit the big time when he joined Paris St Germain in 1991. Ginola helped them win the French Championship, three domestic cups and reach European semi-finals three years in succession, as well as being awarded the French Footballer of the Year title in 1994. He earned the title "El Magnifico" for his brilliant solo performances in Europe against Real Madrid and Barcelona, and was eventually sold to Newcastle for £2.5

million in the summer of 1995.

Ginola made a huge impression on the Geordie fans and was an instant hit, but by the time Kenny Dalglish took over from Kevin Keegan as manager at the start of 1997, he had decided to leave. Spurs paid £2 million to bring him to White Hart Lane in July 1997 and Ginola soon linked up with former Newcastle team-mates Ruel Fox and Les Ferdinand.

David GINOLA

Born: 21 July 1967
Birthplace: Gassin, France
Ht: 5ft 11in
Wt: 11st 10lb
Signed for Spurs: 15 July 1997 for £2 million
Career:
1984–87 Sporting Club de Toulon, 1987–90 Matra Racing, 1990–91 Brest, 1991–95 Paris St Germain, 1995–97 Newcastle United, 1997–present Spurs
Honours:
French League title 1994, French Cup 1993 and 1995, French League Cup 1992, French Footballer of the Year 1994, 16 French caps

---

José **Dominguez**

The diminutive Portuguese winger was signed by Spurs in a surprise move shortly before the start of the 1997–98 season, completing a return to England after two years in his native Lisbon. Dominguez, who measures only 5 feet 4 inches, spent 18 months with Birmingham City from 1994 to 1995 after being signed from Benfica for a bargain price of £180,000 as a teenager. Despite his small frame, he impressed with his skill on the ball and won Under-21 honours before being taken back to Portugal with Sporting Lisbon.

At Sporting, Dominguez gained valuable experience in Europe, in the UEFA Cup and Cup-winners' Cup, and progressed to the full international side. It was during a friendly against England, when he went on as substitute to turn the game by setting up an equalizing goal, that Dominguez was noticed by Gerry Francis. It was a year later that the player signed for Spurs for £1.6 million.

Dominguez is quick, tricky and very skilful and can play on either wing or in the middle behind the strikers.

José DOMINGUEZ

Born: 16 February 1974
Birthplace: Lisbon, Portugal
Ht: 5ft 4 in
Wt: 10st 6lb
Signed for Spurs: 8 Aug 1997 for £1.6 million
Career:
1991–94 Benfica, 1994–95 Birmingham, 1995–97 Sporting Lisbon, 1997–present Spurs

Chapter 8

The Stars of the Future

The stars of the future are as important to any club as the stars of today. Spurs are no exception, and they are proud of a long tradition of bringing through their own players. Many of the clubs stars began this way

FOR a club with a reputation as big spenders, Tottenham have produced a surprising number of outstanding players from their own youth system.

Going right back to the pre-war years, two of the club's greatest managers came through the ranks. Arthur Rowe and Bill Nicholson both started and finished their playing days with Tottenham.

Since the 1960s and the abolition of the maximum wage for players, money has played an increasingly influential part in football and transfer fees have continued to rise higher and higher.

Like many clubs, Tottenham have realised the importance of bringing through their own players. From Steve Perryman, Graeme Souness and Glenn Hoddle in the 1970s to Nick Barmby, Ian Walker and Sol Campbell more recently, the Spurs youth set-up has paid dividends over the years. Not only has the club saved millions in transfer fees, but it has pro-

duced a stream of young talent that has graced British football, if not at White Hart Lane then elsewhere.

Norwich have long been beneficiaries of the Spurs youth system, reaching giddy heights in Europe with a team that included several players who learned their trade at Tottenham, but had to move on to find fame.

Now that transfer fees have spiralled almost beyond control, the need for clubs to produce their own stars has increased the emphasis on youth policy. Once again Spurs are among the leaders, with a steady supply of outstanding talent waiting in the wings.

Manchester United are the most successful club at bringing through top youngsters, but they only beat Spurs in the 1995 FA Youth Cup final in a penalty shoot-out. It is a competition Spurs have won three times: in 1970 (with a side featuring Perryman and Souness), in 1974, and then in 1990 when Ian Walker was in goal.

Promising young players are initially spotted by a national network of scouts and invited to White Hart Lane for trials. The best youngsters between 12 and 16 are asked to join as associated schoolboys, and train in the evenings after school.

Spurs have their own centre of excellence, and several players, Walker, Campbell and Barmby among them, are graduates of the FA's National School of Excellence at Lilleshall, which is to be closed in the near future.

Once they reach the school-leaving age of 16 the best dozen youngsters are taken on as YTS trainees, on a two year development programme, and the pick of the bunch are eventually offered professional contracts.

The club runs two youth teams as well as reserve and Under-19 sides made up mostly of youngsters. The junior side play in the South-East Counties League Division Two, and includes first-year trainees as well as associated schoolboys from time to time.

In their second year, the trainees move up to play in the South-East Counties League Division One. The club has been successful at youth level, but as youth team coach Bob Arber is quick to point out: "Results are great to get at the time, but the real achievement is producing players with good habits and technique, as well as a desire to win, who eventually go on to play in our first team alongside the likes of Sol Campbell and Ian Walker".

Only a few of the intake from any one year will make it through to the first team, but players often go to other clubs and progress from there.

Despite the wealth of multi-million pound talent in the current squad, several of the best young players have been given a chance to show what they can do. This was perhaps the most positive development to have emerged from the injury-hit 1996–97 season. Here are the names to watch out for in the seasons yet to come.

Rory **Allen**

Rory Allen burst on to the scene in spectacular style on his full debut in September 1996 – just six months after turning professional – when he scored against Newcastle at White Hart Lane. He went on to score four goals in 16 games.

Given his chance by injuries to Chris Armstrong and Teddy Sheringham, Allen progressed from youth team football right through to the England Under-21 squad in rapid time.

As a regular in the Spurs side for much of the season, he only missed out on the World Youth Championships in Malaysia in 1997 because of a persistent ankle injury that required surgery at the end of the season. Bright, alert and with an instinct for goal, his finest performance was when he scored twice in a 3-0 Coca-Cola Cup win over Preston.

> **Rory ALLEN**
>
> **Born:** 17 October 1977, Beckenham, London
> **Ht:** 5ft 11in
> **Wt:** 11st 2lbs
> **Position:** Forward

One to watch for the future, Rory Allen made a spectacular start with a goal against Newcastle on his full debut

Garry **Brady**

Scottish midfielder Garry Brady had yet to make his debut by the end of the 1996–97 season, although he was on the substitutes' bench a number of times and is set for a breakthrough into Premiership football.

Brady joined as a trainee as far back as July 1992 and was upgraded to full professional a year later. A regular in the reserves and a Scotland youth player, he is someone of whom much is expected.

His favoured position is as anchor-man in midfield, but he has shown his versatility by playing at full-back and wide midfield when required.

> **Garry BRADY**
>
> **Born:** 7 September 1976, Glasgow
> **Ht:** 5ft 10in
> **Wt:** 10st 5lbs
> **Position:** Midfield
> **Honours:** Scotland schoolboy and youth caps

Stephen **Carr**

After his Premiership debut at Ipswich as a 17-year-old under Ossie Ardiles, Stephen Carr had to wait three more years to make his home debut. Injury and loss of form kept him out of the side in the intervening three seasons, but 1996–97 saw the young Irishman emerge as a first-team regular at White Hart Lane.

Carr was just 17 and had not yet signed as a professional when he made his debut, at Burnley in the League Cup in September 1993. He played one more game, at

Ipswich, but then had a long wait for another chance, although he won the Sidney Wale Challenge Cup as the club's Young Player of the Year in 1994. Once in the side, he quickly became a favourite with the fans for his commitment and never-say-die attitude, and grew stronger as the season wore on.

Having started as an old-fashioned right-back, he became a right-sided wing-back in Ireland's Under-21 side and did the same for Spurs when Gerry Francis changed formation during the 1996–97 season.

Strong in the tackle, fearless and a useful crosser of the ball, Carr has progressed rapidly and looks set to become a regular fixture in the side.

Stephen CARR

Born: 29 August 1976, Dublin
Ht: 5ft 9in
Wt: 12st 4lbs
Position: Full-back
Honours: Ireland Schoolboy, Youth and Under-21 caps

Jamie Clapham

Left-back Jamie Clapham made his league debut on loan for Leyton Orient in February 1997 and followed up a few months later with his full debut for Spurs in the final game of that season, against Coventry.

Clapham made such an impression at Orient that the neighbouring club tried to sign him, but Spurs did not consider letting him go. He also gained league experience during a loan spell with Bristol Rovers towards the end of that season.

He was originally a left-winger when he arrived at Spurs but has been converted into an attacking left-back who provides valuable cover in that position.

Jamie CLAPHAM

Born: 7 December 1975, Lincoln
Ht: 5ft 9in
Wt: 10st 11lbs
Position: Full-back

Stephen Clemence

Son of former Spurs, Liverpool and England goalkeeper Ray, Stephen Clemence has a lot to live up to, but has already shown the talent and maturity to suggest he can match his famous father's achievements .

Clemence was born in Liverpool the year after his father helped the Reds win their first European Cup, but moved south when Ray signed for Spurs in 1981.

Like Barmby, Walker and Campbell, he was a graduate of the FA's National School of Excellence at Lilleshall, where he shone as a gifted midfielder, going on to play for England's school and youth sides before signing professional forms with Spurs in April 1995. He made his full debut on the opening day of the 1997–98 season with an impressive display against Manchester United, and great things are expected of him.

Stephen CLEMENCE

Born: 31 March 1978, Liverpool
Ht: 5ft 11in
Wt: 11st 7lbs
Position: Midfield
Honours: England Schoolboy, Youth and Under-16 caps

Ross Darcy

An outstanding schoolboy footballer in his native Ireland, Ross Darcy is a commanding central defender who has played for his country at all junior levels and played for a representative Irish "B" side despite not yet having made his first-team debut at Spurs.

He has come through the ranks alongside fellow-countryman Kevin Maher, and emulated his defensive partner by winning the Sidney Wale Challenge Cup, named after the club's late chairman, as the best young player at Tottenham in the 1995–96 season. –making him the third Irish player to win the award in successive years, following in the footsteps of Steve Carr and Maher.

That year Darcy captained the youth team to victory in the South-East Counties League Cup .

Ross DARCY

Born: 21 March 1978, Dublin
Ht: 6ft 1in
Wt: 12st 2lbs
Position: Defender
Honours: Republic of Ireland Schoolboy, Youth, Under-21 and "B" caps

Neale Fenn

Local boy Neale Fenn had a baptism of fire when an injury to Teddy Sheringham thrust him into the Spurs attack alongside fellow-teenager Rory Allen in the FA Cup third-round tie against Manchester United at Old Trafford in January 1997.

But the youngster refused to be overawed by the occasion and showed some neat touches against some of the Premiership's best defenders.

Neale Fenn proved Spurs have plenty of young striking talent with his promising performances in 1997

Fenn did not make his League debut for another three months, at Sheffield Wednesday, but he showed enough in the final few games of the season to suggest that he could be a force to be reckoned with in the next few years.

Although he was born in England, Fenn chose to play for his mother's country and has represented the Republic of Ireland at all junior levels, making his Under-21 debut in 1997. He also played for them in the World Youth Championships in Malaysia, scoring against Morocco as the Irish squad finished in a highly impressive third place.

Strong, skilful and with an eye for goal, he may eventually see his partnership with Rory Allen blossom in the Premiership.

Neale FENN

Born: 18 January 1977, Edmonton
Ht: 5 ft 10in
Wt: 12st 8lbs
Position: Forward
Honours: Ireland Schoolboy, Youth and Under-21 caps

Mark **Gower**

Another local boy, Mark Gower had yet to make his first-team breakthrough by the start of the 1997–98 season but is widely regarded as the most natural successor to Glenn Hoddle in the Spurs side.

The gifted midfielder has won rave reviews for his ability on the ball and with application could

Mark GOWER

Born: 5 October 1978, Edmonton
Position: Midfield
Honours: England Schoolboy, Under-16 and Youth caps

become the best home-grown midfielder since Hoddle came through the ranks in the mid-1970s.

Another graduate of the FA's National School of Excellence, he has suffered from a range of injuries but signed professional forms with Spurs in March 1997 and could be set for a glittering career.

Kevin **Maher**

Like his team-mate and defensive partner Ross Darcy, Maher has represented Ireland at all junior levels despite not having played a first-team game for Spurs. He joined as a trainee in 1993 and turned professional a year later. He won the Sidney Wale Trophy, named after Spurs' late chairman, as the club's outstanding young player in 1994–95 after leading the youth side to the South-East Counties League title and FA Youth Cup final, lost in a penalty shoot-out to Manchester United. A strong central defender, great expectations rest on his young shoulders.

Kevin MAHER

Born: 17 October 1976, Ilford
Ht: 6ft
Wt: 12st 5lbs
Position: Defender
Honours: Republic of Ireland Schoolboy, Youth, Under-21 and "B" caps

Paul **McVeigh**

Belfast-born Paul McVeigh made a dramatic entrance on to the Premiership stage at the tail end of the 1996–97 season, taking the field in the final three games of the season and displaying the confidence of an old hand.

His goal in the final game of the season, against Coventry, was scant reward for the boldness he showed despite being dwarfed by most defenders he faced. At just 5ft 6ins, McVeigh is one of the smallest Spurs players to have emerged in the past few years, but he makes up for his lack of height with an ability to run at defenders and find the net.

McVeigh represented Northern Ireland at Youth level after turning professional with Spurs in July 1996 and is expected to acquire full international honours before too long.

Paul McVEIGH

Born: 6 December 1977, Belfast
Ht: 5ft 6in
Wt: 10st 5lbs
Position: Forward
Honours: Northern Ireland Youth caps

Chapter 9

The Great Matches

Every supporter has a favourite game that stands out in the mind, but few fans agree on which Spurs match was the greatest or why.

GOING BACK a generation Spurs fans reserve a special place in their hearts for the 1981 FA Cup Final replay, with Ricky Villa's magical winning goal, or the 1984 UEFA Cup triumph and Tony Parks' match-winning penalty save.

Sometimes, it is a battle against the odds that makes it special, such as the 1991 FA Cup semi-final win over Arsenal, although the fact that it was against the old enemy guaranteed it a place in the hall of fame.

The Premiership years have offered plenty of games that are already part of the club's history. Ronny Rosenthal's hat-trick at Southampton in the FA Cup, and that famous victory at Anfield in the sixth round in 1995 were special games for all Spurs supporters.

In this chapter we present what we consider to be ten of the most memorable games of the past five years. Some fans will be disappointed to find that their favourite game has not been included, while others will think of other magical moments such as Jürgen Klinsmann's spectacular overhead goal on his home debut, or the thrilling 3–1 win over Blackburn later that season. But whether your choice is covered here or not, read on and remember what it felt like to be a Spurs supporter after one of those great days.

Dean Austin beats Ian Rush to the ball with Neil Ruddock – now at Liverpool – looking on

31 October 1992
FA Premier League
TOTTENHAM HOTSPUR 2
LIVERPOOL 0

Until his goal for Real Zaragoza against Arsenal in the 1995 European Cup-winners' Cup final, Nayim's greatest strike was his sensational volley that sent Liverpool on their way to defeat in November 1992.

Spurs fans knew what the Spanish-Moroccan midfielder could do, but his goals were too few and far between for a player of his ability. But he more than made up for the lack of quantity with a strike of pure quality against mighty Liverpool.

Spurs had started the second season of the Premier League in terrible form, winning only two of their first

13 games before meeting Liverpool. Confidence was low but the visit of the Merseysiders was just the sort of big game that Tottenham always seem to lift themselves for, however indifferent their form.

The first half was a tense affair, with neither side seriously threatening to score, and the second half continued in the same vein.

But then midway through the second half the game exploded into life. Nayim had been playing wide on the left in his usual role, but he drifted into the centre of the pitch just in time to pick up a loose clearance. Without breaking stride he hit a superb looping volley from all of 40 yards which flew over the head of a startled Bruce Grobbelaar in the Liverpool goal, all but bursting the roof of the net.

It was immediately hailed as one of the greatest strikes ever seen at White Hart Lane and deservedly won the BBC's "Goal of the Month" competition.

The goal put Spurs firmly in the driving seat, and they sealed victory ten minutes later when Neil Ruddock went up into the opposing penalty area for a corner and sent a thumping header past the bemused Grobbelaar.

Ruddock was ever-present that season, having returned from Southampton the previous year for his second spell at the club. But it was to be a brief stay as he left in the summer of 1993 – for Liverpool!

> **TOTTENHAM 2**
> **LIVERPOOL 0 (ht 0 – 0)**
>
> **Venue:**
> White Hart Lane
> **Att:**
> 32,917
> **Tottenham:**
> Thorstvedt, Austin, Ruddock, Mabbutt, Edinburgh, Allen, Sedgley, Nayim, Sheringham, Durie, Barmby (Turner)
> **Spurs' Goalscorers:**
> Nayim, Ruddock

7 March 1993
FA Cup Sixth Round
MANCHESTER CITY 2
TOTTENHAM HOTSPUR 4

For years Manchester City had been something of a bogey side for Spurs, so there was some apprehension when the sixth-round draw led to Maine Road. Spurs were starting to show good form, with the combination of youngster Nick Barmby and new signing Teddy Sheringham really blossoming in attack. The ammunition was supplied by Darren Anderton, who was finally showing what he could do following a hernia operation to get him fully fit after a quiet start to his Spurs career.

Manchester City fans tried (and failed) to get the FA Cup sixth-round tie abandoned. Spurs won 4–2

With those three on top of their game, Spurs had gone on a run of five successive League wins from the end of January, winning Doug Livermore the Manager of the Month award for February.

But it had all come crashing down at Sheffield United with a 6–0 defeat by Dave Bassett's men, and questions were being asked about Tottenham's appetite for the cup game. All doubts were soon dispelled, however, as Spurs put on an imperious show to destroy City in a match that was televised live.

Spurs started well but it was City who took the lead when Mike Sheron scored after only ten minutes. The forecasters of doom were in their element as it looked as if Spurs were to suffer again at Maine Road. But then Nayim got in on the act, hitting a hat-trick, his only one for Spurs. His first was a well-placed shot after a good move in the 25th minute to put Spurs level.

Spurs then gained the psychological advantage when Steve Sedgley put them ahead a minute before half-time, a rare goal for the versatile player. It was a huge boost for Spurs and clearly had a demoralising effect on City, as Nayim scored again early in the second half.

By now the home supporters were getting restless and, when Nayim scored again in the 86th minute to make it 4–1, they stormed on to the pitch. Mounted police were called in to clear the playing surface and

Steve Sedgley celebrates his goal in the 4–2 FA Cup Final win at Maine Road

Sheringham stepped up to take the penalty, only to blast it over the bar.

It was even suggested afterwards that the shrewd striker had missed deliberately to avoid infuriating the City fans any more, although their anger was reserved mostly for their own players.

The trouble overshadowed the result briefly, but when the dust settled the only important thing was that Spurs were in the semi-final of the FA Cup. But just as Spurs fans started dreaming of another Wembley triumph, deadly rivals Arsenal won through to beat them in the semi-final and get revenge for their 3–1 defeat at the same stage two years earlier.

> **MANCHESTER CITY 2**
> **TOTTENHAM 4 (ht 1 – 2)**
>
> **FA Cup**
> **Venue:**
>   Maine Road
> **Att:** 34,050
> **Tottenham:**
>   Thorstvedt, Austin, Mabbutt, Ruddock, Edinburgh, Anderton (Turner), Allen, Sedgley, Nayim, Samways, Sheringham.
> **Spurs' Goalscorers:**
>   Nayim (3), Sedgley

25 August 1993
FA Premier League
LIVERPOOL 1
TOTTENHAM HOTSPUR 2

Victories at Anfield have always been a rare event for Tottenham sides, but when new manager Ossie Ardiles took his side to beat Liverpool it started to look as if Spurs had a side capable of making it a habit.

Not only that but, following the opening-day win at Newcastle and victory over Manchester City, there was genuine optimism that Tottenham could make a serious title challenge for the first time in years.

Ultimately it was not to be, and indeed Spurs ended up battling against the very real threat of relegation by the end of the season. A lot of their problems were due to the fact that Teddy Sheringham was injured badly in a clash with Manchester United's Bryan Robson in October and did not play until the final few games of the season.

> **LIVERPOOL 1**
> **TOTTENHAM 2 (ht 0 – 0)**
>
> **Venue:**
>   Anfield
> **Att:**
>   42,456
> **Tottenham:**
>   Thorstvedt, Austin, Calderwood, Mabbutt, Campbell, Sedgley, Howells (Caskey), Samways, Dozzell, Sheringham, Durie.
> **Spurs' Goalscorer:**
>   Sheringham 2 (1 pen)

when calm was restored, play continued. City's Republic of Ireland full-back Terry Phelan scored an amazing solo goal, running half the length of the field.

The action did not stop there, however. Young winger Andy Turner, on as a substitute for Darren Anderton, was tripped in the penalty area and Teddy

Spurs relied heavily on Sheringham's goals, as he proved in a superb performance at Anfield. In what was a pulsating match from start to finish, Liverpool took the lead in the 18th minute when Nigel Clough, recently signed from Nottingham Forest, shot home past Erik Thorstvedt.

It was a setback for Spurs, but Sheringham was in determined mood. He was playing against his good friend and former team-mate Neil Ruddock, who had left Spurs for Liverpool that summer in an acrimonious move. Ruddock was roundly booed by the vast army of travelling Spurs fans every time he touched the ball, and could do nothing to stop Sheringham. The England striker equalized for Spurs on the half-hour when he was pushed over in the penalty area as he jockeyed for position.

Sheringham had no qualms about taking the penalty in the fevered atmosphere, thumping the ball into the net to silence the Kop and send the Spurs fans into raptures of delight.

Then, three minutes before half-time, came the killer blow for Liverpool as Sheringham got the ball inside the penalty area, kept his nerve and tucked the ball away for what proved to be the winning goal.

Again because of the timing of the goal, the psychological edge had swung to Spurs. Although Liverpool attacked intensively in the second half, the Tottenham defence held out magnificently, with skipper Gary Mabbutt and Ruddock's replacement, Colin Calderwood, in defiant mood.

Teddy Sheringham punches the air in delight after scoring at Anfield. He got both Spurs' goals that day

5 May 1994
FA Premier League

OLDHAM 0
TOTTENHAM HOTSPUR 2

When Tottenham fans look back at the trouble 1993–94 season, the 2–0 win at Oldham may not stand out as the most stylish victory – but it was certainly the most important.

Spurs travelled to Boundary Park needing a win to avoid getting drawn into serious trouble at the foot of the table. It was a real relegation clash, with both sides desperate for the points that would go a long way to guaranteeing Premiership survival.

Spurs had hammered Oldham at home in September, with a three-goal burst from Steve Sedgley and Teddy Sheringham in the opening ten minutes setting up a comfortable 5–0 win. But eight months later at Boundary Park it was a different matter as Spurs had to dig out a performance of guts and determination to win.

The match had been postponed twice at short notice and was finally played on a Thursday night, live on television. The pitch was in a poor state, with little grass but plenty of sand, and it was a cold wet night at one of English football's most exposed grounds.

It was clearly not going to be a night for the faint-hearted, and those Spurs fans who had made the long journey from London for the third time were in defiant mood. Fortunately, so was the team.

With so much at stake it was a typically tense affair, with neither side prepared to take chances. Oldham suffered a blow in the opening minute when their captain Mike Milligan had to go off after a clash of heads with Kevin Scott.

But Spurs eventually made the breakthrough in the 37th minute when Ronny Rosenthal made space in the penalty area and set up Vinny Samways to curl a low shot past Oldham keeper Paul Gerrard. It was just the boost Spurs needed and sapped the confidence of the Oldham players.

Spurs continued to dominate but were

Vinny Samways' most important goal: it secured victory over Oldham and eased relegation fears

uncomfortable with a slender one-goal lead in such a vital game. As often happens when fate lends a hand, Spurs had a major slice of luck when the ball was cleared off the line in the 77th minute. Tottenham immediately took the ball to the other end of the pitch and scored the goal that sealed victory. Gerrard failed to hold a long shot from Dean Austin and David Howells followed up to put the loose ball home, calming nerves for the final 12 minutes as Spurs hung on to survive while Oldham were ultimately relegated.

20 August 1994
FA Premiership

SHEFFIELD WEDNESDAY 3
TOTTENHAM HOTSPUR 4

If there had been any doubts about the impact Jürgen Klinsmann would have on the Premiership they were blown away in spectacular style on the opening day of the 1994 season.

No one could have failed to ignore the impact Klinsmann made after he inspired Spurs to victory at Sheffield Wednesday, with every newspaper showing

---

**OLDHAM ATHLETIC 0
TOTTENHAM 2 (ht 0 – 1)**

Venue:
Boundary Park

Att:
14,283

Tottenham:
Thorstvedt, Austin, Sedgley, Scott, Mabbutt, Edinburgh, Samways, Howells, Nethercott, Sheringham, Rosenthal (Dozzell).

Spurs' Goalscorers:
Samways, Howells

Jürgen Klinsmann met all expectations, heading the winner on his Spurs debut at Sheffield Wednesday

the diving celebrations by all 11 players after Teddy Sheringham's opening goal. It was Klinsmann's way of responding to the suggestions that he was a "diver" in the penalty box, and there were to be many more celebrations before the season ended.

But back to that opening day. Ossie Ardiles was bold in his plans as he unleashed the "Famous Five" – Klinsmann, Sheringham, Darren Anderton, Nick Barmby and Ilie Dumitrescu.

It was an attacking line-up that was the envy of the Premiership, and it soon made its mark. Sheringham opened the scoring after 17 minutes when he latched on to a mistake by Dan Petrescu to curl a fantastic shot past Kevin Pressman with the outside of his right boot. Spurs made it 2–0 on the half-hour when Anderton exchanged passes with Sheringham, whose return was so well disguised that the winger had a free run at goal

before prodding the ball into the bottom corner.

Wednesday pulled a goal back 21 minutes into the second half when Petrescu made up for his defensive slip by stabbing the ball past Ian Walker. The game was level just 24 minutes from the end when Spurs defender Colin Calderwood swept the ball into his own net as he tried to stop Chris Bart-Williams latching on to Mark Bright's pass. Nick Barmby put Spurs

SHEFFIELD WED 3 TOTTENHAM 4 (ht 0 – 2)
Venue: Hillsborough
Att: 34,051
Tottenham: Walker, Kerslake, Edinburgh, Campbell (Mabbutt), Nethercott, Anderton, Barmby, Calderwood, Dumitrescu (Hazard), Klinsmann, Sheringham.
Spurs' Goalscorers: Sheringham, Anderton, Barmby, Klinsmann

Ronny Rosenthal scores the second goal of a fabulous hat-trick to transform the FA Cup tie at the Dell

back into the lead almost immediately with a thrilling shot into the far corner of the net after picking up Sheringham's back header and running at the Wednesday defence.

With eight minutes to go Spurs fans saw the goal they wanted when David Kerslake's centre was headed in powerfully by a leaping Jürgen Klinsmann.

To complete a dramatic afternoon for the German striker, he was then taken off on a stretcher after a sickening clash of heads with Wednesday defender Des Walker. David Hirst's brilliant volley in the closing stages only served to frustrate Wednesday – it was Tottenham's and Klinsmann's day.

1 March 1995
FA Cup Fifth Round replay
SOUTHAMPTON 2
TOTTENHAM HOTSPUR 6

This is the game that will forever be remembered as Ronny Rosenthal's finest hour.

The Israeli international, never the most prolific of strikers during his Tottenham career, hit a sensational hat-trick to inspire Spurs to an amazing comeback.

When "Rocket" Ronny was sent on as a substitute shortly before half-time in this fifth-round FA Cup replay, Spurs were 2–0 down and seemingly out of the cup.

Rosenthal – the "Super-Sub" – transformed the game with two goals to take it into extra time. He completed his hat-trick as Spurs eventually ran out 6–2 winners against a shell-shocked Southampton.

It had all seemed to be going Southampton's way when they went ahead after five minutes. Jim Magilton rolled the ball wide to Jason Dodd, who crossed towards the far post for Neil Shipperley to steer the ball past Walker. Southampton scored again after 35 minutes. Dean Austin hacked down winger Neil Heaney in the penalty area and Le Tissier scored from the penalty spot.

Rosenthal was then introduced as substitute a minute before half-time, with Gerry Francis ordering him to "take the intitiative". He did so in spectacular

High drama as Jürgen Klinsmann scores a last-minute winner at Anfield in the FA Cup sixth round

11 March 1995
FA Cup Sixth Round
LIVERPOOL 1
TOTTENHAM HOTSPUR 2

Tottenham victories at Anfield have been rare enough over the years, but to win an FA Cup sixth-round tie with a goal in the dying minutes was something really special.

For Jürgen Klinsmann, who hit that late winner, it was the high point of his Spurs career and an emotional day. The German striker left the pitch in tears, overwhelmed by the emotion of the occasion, and it was a day that will live long in the memory of the fans lucky enough to be there.

Even the Liverpool fans applauded Spurs off the pitch after one of the most dramatic and exciting games seen at any English ground for years. It was a match that had everything: skill, commitment, tension and high drama.

Spurs had failed to beat Liverpool in six previous FA Cup matches but they were in confident mood after the amazing 6–2 win over Southampton in the previous round and knew that an upset could be on the cards.

Gerry Francis had turned the side's fortunes around after taking over from Ossie Ardiles four months earlier, and the new Spurs were fitter, leaner and defensively meaner.

Right from the kick-off, the game was played at a cracking pace and Klinsmann might have scored as early as the second minute when a flicked header from Sheringham put him clear.

His shot was deflected away by goalkeeper David James and instead it was Liverpool who took the lead, seven minutes before half time. Winger Mark Walters centred to the near post where prolific striker Robbie Fowler nipped in to head home.

If that was well-crafted, Tottenham's equalizer a couple of minutes later was clinical. David Howells started the move with a raking forward ball to Klinsmann, who placed a perfect pass in the path of Teddy Sheringham. The England striker ran on to the ball and curled an inch-perfect shot past James from the edge of the penalty area.

Despite chances for Walters and McManaman, Spurs had a better hold on the game than their opponents, and their extra training started to pay off. The longer the game went on, the more Liverpool tired and Spurs grew stronger. Then, with only a minute to

style, scoring after 56 minutes when he drilled home a cross from Nick Barmby. The goal gave Spurs hope, and when Rosenthal equalized two minutes later by firing home a thundering drive from 25 yards after a mazy dribble from the right, the game went into extra time.

Now Spurs were in command, and Rosenthal completed his hat-trick after 101 minutes with a marvellous shot from 20 yards that gave goalkeeper Bruce Grobbelaar no chance.

Teddy Sheringham was sent clear by Jürgen Klinsmann to score the fourth goal before Barmby gave Southampton's defence the slip and rounded Grobbelaar to slot home the fifth. In the final minute of the game Barmby lured the Southampton keeper out of his area before squaring to Darren Anderton to slide home the sixth.

It was one of the most dramatic comebacks in the history of the FA Cup, and a night that belonged, quite rightly, to "Rocket" Ronny Rosenthal.

SOUTHAMPTON 2
TOTTENHAM 6
(after extra-time – score at 90 mins 2 – 2)

Venue:
The Dell

Att:
15,172

Tottenham:
Walker, Austin, Mabbutt, Calderwood, Edinburgh, Nethercott (Rosenthal), Anderton, Howells, Barmby, Klinsmann, Sheringham.

Spurs' Goalscorers:
Rosenthal (3), Sheringham, Barmby, Anderton

go and a replay looming, Klinsmann ran on to a perfect flick from Sheringham and slid the ball past onrushing 'keeper David James for the winning goal.

Anfield was stunned, the Spurs fans were jubilant and, when the final whistle went moments later, Gerry Francis celebrated on the pitch with Klinsmann and the rest the players. Even Liverpool manager Roy Evans admitted: "It was a cracking game of football".

For a time it looked like Tottenham's name was on the cup, but as the semi-final defeat against Everton was to prove, it was not to be.

LIVERPOOL 1
TOTTENHAM 2 (ht 1 – 1)

Venue:
Anfield
Att:
39,592
Tottenham:
Walker, Edinburgh, Calderwood, Austin, Mabbutt, Rosenthal, Anderton, Barmby, Howells, Klinsmann, Sheringham.
Spurs' Goalscorers:
Sheringham, Klinsmann

---

1 January 1996
FA Premiership
TOTTENHAM HOTSPUR 4
MANCHESTER UTD 1

What a way to start the new year! Spurs shocked the Premiership and announced their genuine title aspirations with a thumping win over United, who were to win the title again that season.

Spurs had moved into the top five in November and were to stay there until March, when a poor run of only two wins in the last nine games cost them a place in Europe by one point on the final day. Although Spurs were in a rich vein of form, the manner of victory and margin of defeat was still surprising, coming as it did against England's most consistently effective team.

Optimism was high at White Hart Lane as Alex Ferguson brought his men to Tottenham for the big televised game on New Year's Day. United were giving a trial to French defender William Prunier, but the central defender looked out of his depth against a rampant Spurs attack.

Teddy Sheringham and Chris Armstrong were scoring freely in a partnership that was to be worth 46 goals that season, and they tore United's defence apart.

Spurs were much the better side from the start and the only surprise was that it took them 34 minutes to make the breakthrough, when Armstrong split the United defence with a brilliant pass and Sheringham

scored from six yards.

Barely 60 seconds had elapsed before the scores were level again, with Phil Neville crossing for Andy Cole to score United's equalizer.

But Sol Campbell restored Tottenham's advantage on the stroke of half-time when he blasted the ball home after Sheringham headed down a Dean Austin cross into his path.

United goalkeeper Peter Schmeichel had been injured in the warm-up but played throughout the first half, only to be replaced by Kevin Pilkington at half time. The substitute 'keeper fared no better than his senior, and his first job was to pick the ball out of the net after a Chris Armstrong stooping header from a Ronny Rosenthal cross.

United threatened a brief fight-back, but Armstrong ended their hopes in the 65th minute when he scored a classic glancing header from Sheringham's cross to complete a famous victory.

TOTTENHAM 4
MAN UNITED 1 (ht 2 – 1)

Venue:
White Hart Lane
Att:
32,852
Tottenham:
Walker, Austin, Nethercott, Calderwood, Edinburgh, Dumitrescu (McMahon), Caskey, Campbell, Rosenthal, Sheringham, Armstrong.
Spurs' Goalscorers:
Sheringham, Campbell, Armstrong (2)

---

2 May 1996
FA Premiership
LEEDS 1
TOTTENHAM HOTSPUR 3

This was the game in which Darren Anderton announced his comeback from serious injury in spectacular style and proved his fitness for England's bid to win Euro '96.

Anderton had missed most of the season with a succession of groin and hernia problems, and looked like he would not be fit enough to make the England squad. But he had worked hard to get fit and it paid off in a remarkable performance capped with two fine goals that convinced England coach Terry Venables that Anderton could not be overlooked.

Struggling Leeds – missing eight regulars through injury – surprisingly took the lead after 13 minutes when Gary Kelly's cross was headed home by David Wetherall. Anderton then flashed a shot wide before Teddy Sheringham forced a good save from former

Teddy Sheringham and Chris Armstrong celebrate during Spurs' 4–1 demolition of Manchester United

Arsenal 'keeper John Lukic, so it was no surprise when Spurs equalized on 18 minutes. Sheringham headed Ruel Fox's corner back into the goalmouth and Chris Armstrong volleyed home his 22nd and final goal of the season. Armstrong had every reason to be delighted with his tally.

He had been signed from Crystal Palace for a club record £4.5m the previous summer and had the difficult task of following in Jürgen Klinsmann's footsteps. He found goals hard to come by at first, but once he started scoring he got into the habit and his partner-ship with Sheringham was worth 46 goals, second only to Robbie Fowler and Stan Collymore at Liverpool that season.

Once Armstrong had equalized at Elland Road Spurs took control, and they went ahead midway through the first half.

Once again Sheringham was the provider, his long pass sending Anderton through. On only his second start since returning to the side, the England midfielder showed great poise and confidence in beating goalkeeper John Lukic.

Spurs turned on the style, and a well-deserved third goal midway through the second half completed their first double over Leeds since 1980. Once again Anderton supplied the finishing touch when he linked with Sheringham and collected the return pass before beating Lukic from six yards.

It was proof that he was back to his best, and he and Sheringham went on to play in all of England's games as they went so close to reaching the final of Euro '96.

**LEEDS 1
TOTTENHAM 3 (ht 1–2)**

Venue:
Elland Road
Att:
30,061
Tottenham:
Walker, Edinburgh, Campbell, Mabbut, Wilson, Anderton, Dozzell, Howells, Fox, Sheringham, Armstrong.
Spurs' Goalscorers:
Anderton (2), Armstrong

**4 March 1997
FA Premiership**

SUNDERLAND 0
TOTTENHAM 4

This was the game in which Steffen Iversen finally fulfilled the promise he had shown since signing from Rosenborg of Trondheim the previous December.

The young Norwegian striker had played manfully in place of the injured Chris Armstrong but he had not scored the number of goals he deserved – until he faced Sunderland.

While his former team-mates were playing Juventus in the quarter-finals of the European Cup, Iversen was playing out of his skin at a windswept Roker Park.

With Sunderland struggling to score goals and in the relegation zone, Gerry Francis knew that a good start would be a massive boost – but he could not have anticipated being 2–0 up within ten minutes.

Barely a minute had elapsed when a deep free kick from Colin Calderwood dropped into the penalty area and Iversen showed his poacher's instincts by hooking the loose ball into the net.

The second goal, eight minutes later, was an absolute cracker as another Calderwood free kick was flicked on by Sheringham for Iversen to loft the ball over Sunderland keeper Lionel Perez. The 20-year-old Norwegian striker was only denied a first half hat-trick when his stinging shot was saved by Perez.

Darren Anderton savours the first of two goals against Leeds which proved him fit for Euro '96

Steffen Iversen showed a glimpse of what was to come with a superb hat-trick against Sunderland

The French goalkeeper also denied Darren Anderton at the near post, but could do nothing to stop Allan Nielsen shooting home the third goal after Sheringham and Iversen combined to send him clear.

After half-time Sunderland had only their pride to play for, but it was Spurs and Iversen who were to have the last laugh. His first hat-trick for the club arrived in the 62nd minute when he latched on to a half-hearted clearance to thump in a 25-yard shot that flew past Perez and into the top corner.

It was a much-needed morale boost for Spurs, who had lost seven of their previous nine games, including a 7–1 humiliation at Newcastle. The defeat of Sunderland was the first of a run of three wins in five games that kept Tottenham's hopes of a UEFA Cup place alive until the last few weeks of the season.

For Sunderland, the writing was on the wall, and this result hastened their return to the First Division after just one year in the Premiership.

**SUNDERLAND 0
TOTTENHAM 4 (ht 1–3)**

Venue:
Roker Park
Att:
20,785
Tottenham:
Walker, Scales, Calderwood, Campbell, Austin, Anderton, Howells, Nielsen, Wilson (Carr), Iversen, Sheringham.
Goalscorers:
Iversen (3), Nielsen

Chapter 10
At Home

The club's fortunes on the field are just one part of the huge multi-million pound organization that is Tottenham Hotspur. From £6 in 1887 to millions today, the club has come a long way in terms of turnover as well as goals.

Tottenham Hotspur plc

The 12 schoolboys who founded the club almost 120 years ago with an annual subscription of around sixpence (two and a half pence) each would no doubt be amazed at today's multi-million pound organisation. The days when clubs at the highest level were funded mainly by fans coming though the turnstiles have long gone.

Tottenham's first reported annual profit was just £6 in 1887. 109 years on, that figure had risen to almost £10 million profit from a turnover of around £37.5 million.

In the financial year ending May 1996, gate receipts of more than £13 million accounted for little more than a third of turnover once profit on player sales was taken into account.

Merchandising, sponsorship and television money totalling £11 million accounted for a quarter of the club's income, almost as much as total ticket sales.

White Hart Lane is one of the finest stadiums in Britain and still expanding

In the first five years of the Premiership, Tottenham spent £27 million on stadium redevelopment, raising £12 million for the latest North Stand rebuilding by way of a rights issue.

When a single player can cost £15 million, more than the value of most non-Premiership clubs, the financial stakes are high. And Spurs supporters know more than most that it can all go horribly wrong, after the club nearly went into liquidation in 1991.

The club was originally floated on the stock market in 1983 and raised almost £4 million to clear debts accumulated mostly by rebuilding the West Stand.

Many fans bought shares in the club, more as mementoes than as genuine money-making schemes. But the club ran into more financial problems towards the end of the 1980s after more stadium development, and it took Alan Sugar's buy-out and personal financial undertakings and support to save the club from liquidation.

Now the club is financially secure and profitable and Sugar and Littner are determined not to repeat the mistakes of past administrations (not just at Tottenham) when inflated transfer fees, huge wage-bills and spiralling building costs led clubs to the brink of bankruptcy.

The regular capacity crowds at White Hart Lane and the income from merchandising, sponsorship and television rights mean that Tottenham are able to spend millions on players but still trade as a viable company.

One of the biggest single increases in income came in 1992 when BSkyB bought the rights to televise the Premier League at its inception. The initial deal, worth £205 million over five years, gave a huge boost to Premiership clubs.

The next step forward in commercial terms for clubs is pay-per-view television, with the prospect of individual matches being sold to viewers or a 'season ticket' of televised treats.

With the advent of computer-friendly 'smart-cards' and the potential of digital TV for multi-casting, it is conceivable that the Spurs supporter of the not-too-distant future will have one credit card-sized device for admission to matches, viewing on satellite or cable television, purchases in the club shop and access to the club's own Internet services.

It is a long way from the first paying spectators spending threepence (1p) to watch early games at Northumberland Park, but that is the price of progress.

Changing colours

Tottenham have long been known as the Lillywhites

Changing Designs

1921 - The cockerel motif, within a shield, first appeared on club shirts for the FA Cup final.

1953 - A streamlined design of the cockerel was introduced.

1966 - The cockerel on ball design was first used on the club shirt.

1977 - Spurs first commercial club deal, with Admiral, saw a manufacturer's logo appear on the home kit for the very first time.

1980 - Le Coq Sportif took over shirt manufacture.

1982 - Centenary season kit.

1983 - First shirt sponsor, Holsten, appeared on shirt.

1985 - Manufacturer changed to Hummel.

1991 - Umbro take over kit manufacture, first used in FA cup final.

1995 - Manufacturer changed to Pony and Hewlett Packard took over shirt sponsorship from Holsten.

---

for their trademark white shirts, usually worn with navy blue shorts, but they went through a rainbow of colours in the early years before settling on their famous strip at the turn of the century.

Little changed, apart from shirt collars and length of shorts, for the next 75 years or so, before the revolution in kit design put the replica market uppermost in manufacturers' minds.

With most clubs changing either their first, second or third choice kit every year or so, it seems hard to believe that the strips worn by professional footballers barely changed from decade to decade until the mid-1970s.

Only 20 years ago the white shirt was augmented only by the number on the back and the simple club crest of a cockerel on top of a ball. Now players have their names on the back, the club's sponsors and kit suppliers on the front and the Premiership logo on their sleeves.

It has led to a lucrative market in replica kits, with Spurs selling around 250,000 shirts per year at an average price of £35.

White Hart Lane – the History

Tottenham have come a long way, metaphorically speaking, since they first played just down the road from the magnificent all-seater stadium that is the modern White Hart Lane.

The club's first games, in the 1880s, took place on the public playing fields of Tottenham Marshes and soon started to draw regular crowds of 400 or more.

By 1888, Tottenham decided to find their own ground and relocated to Northumberland Park, a pitch shared with Foxes FC which cost £17 a year to rent. Having their own pitch enabled the club to make an admission charge of threepence (1p) and they took the grand sum of 17 shillings (85p) from the first match there, a reserve game.

Spurs joined the Southern Alliance shortly afterwards and, under the patronage of John Oliver – who later became club president – a small grandstand capable of housing 100 people was built.

Tottenham became a limited company in 1898 and with that leap came the impetus to move to a better ground and to grow as a club.

The opportunity to do that came when the

Manager Gerry Francis welcomes David Ginola after the French winger was signed from Newcastle

Charrington firm of brewers abandoned their plans to build a housing estate behind the White Hart pub on Tottenham High Road. Club directors Charles Roberts and Bob Buckle knew that the football crowds would provide regular trade for the pub and, on the promise that they would attract a minimum of 1,000 spectators per first-team game, a deal was agreed. The former horticultural nursery was converted into what is now White Hart Lane. Mobile stands were brought along from the Northumberland Park site giving cover to 2,500 spectators. The club offices, previously at 808 Tottenham High Road, were also housed in the new enclosure.

The White Hart Lane ground finally opened in September 1899 with the visit of Notts County, who Tottenham crushed 4–1 in front of 5,000 supporters. The receipts from the game amounted to over £115, half of which was paid to the visitors. The first competitive game, a 1–0 win over QPR a week later,

brought in double that amount from a crowd of 11,000.

Early season tickets, priced at 15 shillings (75p) were sold for the main stand, and crowds gradually increased as the ground's capacity rose to 32,000 by 1904.

A year later £2,000 was generated from the sale of shares to contribute towards the cost of over £11,000 to buy the freehold and further land at the north end of the ground

The size of the banking at each end was then increased and extended to take the capacity up to 40,000 and, in 1905, Archibald Leitch, the famous stadium architect was asked to draw up plans for a new main stand.

The imposing West stand took five years to build and was finally opened in September 1909 at the start of the club's first season in the First Division. It seated 5,300 and had a paddock in front for a further 6,000 standing spectators. It was also the first resting place for the club's famous symbol of a cockerel atop a ball, which still remains.

Within two years the East Stand was also covered and the wooden terracing around the ground was replaced by concrete, giving a capacity of 50,000.

It was around this time that people were referring to the ground as White Hart Lane, whereas it had previously been known as the High Road or the White Hart ground.

During the First World War the ground was used as a rifle range and a factory for gas-masks, with 10 million being produced. But far from letting hostilities disrupt the football, the club played their war-time games at nearby Millfields, Clapton and even Highbury.

Spurs returned to White Hart Lane after the war and used the profits from the 1921 FA Cup win to build split-level, covered stands at the Park Lane and Paxton Road ends. This increased the total capacity of the ground to 58,000, with 40,000 under cover.

By 1921 the club had also purchased the Red House at the front of the ground, which had been used as a coffee house and restaurant for many years, and turned it into a club office.

The next major development was the redevelopment of the massive East Stand at a cost of £60,000, an enormous sum at the time and equivalent to the club's total profits in the previous 17 years. Again Leitch was the architect of what was the biggest and most impressive stand in the League, with 5,100 seats and terracing for 18,700 people. It was opened in September 1934, taking the capacity to 78,000, although the club record stands at 75,038 for the FA Cup visit of Sunderland in 1936.

The Second World War brought further disruption, with a reversal of fortune as Arsenal were forced to move up the Seven Sisters Road to use White Hart Lane for their wartime home fixtures.

After six years of war, crowds flocked to White Hart Lane and Spurs had some of the highest attendances in the country. Floodlights were introduced in 1953 and when they were upgraded in 1957, the original famous cockerel had to be moved from the West to the East Stand, but now has a colleague on the West.

By the early 1960s, the Park Lane and Paxton Road stands were fitted with a tier of seats above the terraces, and by 1973 all four stands were finally linked.

Then in November 1980 the old West Stand was knocked down and replaced by the stand which is still in place today, costing over £4 million and providing offices and 72 executive boxes in addition to seating for more than 6,000 spectators. It was officially opened on 6 February 1982 for a match against Wolves.

In July 1989 the East Stand was refurbished but long-time residents of the famous 'Shelf' terracing were appeased as it was left intact when the stand was reopened on October 18 for the visit of Arsenal.

The Shelf was finally converted into seats when the Taylor report requiring Premiership stadiums to be all-seater was implemented in the mid 1990s.

The old South Stand was demolished in 1994 and a new stand completed a year later, incorporating a Jumbotron television screen. The East and West Stand roofs were linked to give a wrap-around effect throughout the whole stadium.

Work to increase the capacity of the North Stand began in the

Manchester Utd and Spurs succeded on the stock market as well

summer of 1997 to add another tier and bring it into line with the rest of the stadium. When finished, it should give White Hart Lane a capacity of around 38,000 – and there are already tentative plans for further re-development.

Showbiz connection

Having established a reputation as London's most glamorous club, there has been an obvious and symbiotic relationship between Spurs and showbusiness.

The club can boast more celebrity fans than most, and it can also point to its own contribution to the world of entertainment over the years with a succession of popular and some not-so-popular records.

Going back to 1961, a group called The Totnamites released a 45-rpm single called "Tip Top Tottenham Hotspur" to celebrate winning the Double. On the B side was their version of "Danny Boy" in tribute to club captain Danny Blanchflower.

The same year saw the release of BBC radio's FA Cup final commentary, although it is hardly likely to have made much impact in the charts!

One of the first football records to be a big hit in the pop charts was "Nice One Cyril" by the Cockerel Chorus. Released in 1973, it was based on the catchphrase used in a popular television advert and picked up on by Spurs fans to sing to Cyril Knowles.

The left-back, now sadly deceased, was one of the crowd's favourite players because of his charismatic personality and attacking instincts and he became a household name after the song reached the Top 20 singles chart. He admitted later that he was thoroughly sick and tired with strangers coming up to him and singing the song almost 20 years on.

Tottenham's next big entry in the charts was "Ossie's Dream", which again made the Top 20 in 1981. By this time most clubs who reached the FA Cup final were recording songs, so it was entirely appropriate that Spurs chose to immortalise Ossie Ardiles' much-stated ambition to win the cup.

"Cockney" entertainers Chas and Dave were enlisted to write and play the song, with the first-team squad singing along in what became one of the best known football songs of all time.

Who can forget the classic line: "Ossie's going to Wembley, his knees have gone all trembley"? Certainly not the thousands of Spurs fans who sang the song over and over again on the night Ricky Villa

lit up Wembley with his famous winning goal against Manchester City.

Chas and Dave were involved the following year as Spurs reached the FA Cup final again, and their song "Tottenham Tottenham" was heard loud and clear as they beat QPR.

It was around this time that Spurs released "The Tottenham Hotspur Party Album", an LP of popular songs adapted to the football world and sung by the players. It was perhaps Glenn Hoddle's solo version of John Lennon's "Happy Xmas, War is Over" that persuaded the Spurs midfielder to negotiate a recording contract with Chris Waddle as his partner.

The result was an album and single called "Diamond Lights" which again reached the charts and featured the pair miming on "Top Of The Pops". It has to be said that neither looked as comfortable on stage as they did on the pitch and, after a less successful follow-up, they sensibly abandoned showbusiness to concentrate on football again.

But the showbiz world has not abandoned Spurs. Over the years a wide range of celebrity fans have been regulars at White Hart Lane.

Warren Mitchell, who played West Ham fanatic Alf Garnett on television, was in fact a season ticketholder at Spurs for many years. The late Peter Cook, arch satirist and comedian, was another lifelong supporter and he even featured in a television advert in the early 1980s, leading the team out of the tunnel at White Hart Lane.

A.J. Ayer, the philosopher, was another Spurs supporter who could be as passionate about Tottenham as he was about metaphysics, but it must have helped that he was an expert in systems of belief.

Spurs supporters have needed a sense of humour over the years, so it is appropriate that comedians such as Bobby Davro and Hale and Pace are fans. Edmonton-born Bruce Forsyth, king of light-entertainers, is another long-standing fan and so is Michael Barrymore, the heir to his throne.

More recent celebrity fans have included controversial columnist and broadcaster Richard Littlejohn, Caesar "the Geezer" from Talk Radio, models Linda Lusardi and Samantha Fox, singer George Michael, and even former England captain Mike Gatting.

It seems that as long as Spurs keep up their glamorous reputation by playing entertaining and attractive football, there will always be other entertainers queuing up to watch them.

The North London Derbies

The fixtures against Arsenal are the first that every Spurs fan looks for on the fixture list at the start of each season.

EVER SINCE 1887 there has been a special relationship with the old enemy, Arsenal – and it has not always been a happy one.

That first meeting between the two sides, just five years after Tottenham's formation and a year after Arsenal started life as Dial Square, was called off with 15 minutes to go because Arsenal's players complained of poor light, an excuse more regularly associated with cricket.

Not surprisingly, they were trailing 2–1 at the time and the 'result' was nullified. It did, however, set the tone for the meetings between the sides over the next 110 or so years.

Few other fixtures in Britain, possibly the world, match the intensity of the North London derby, although an older generation of Spurs fans still regard Arsenal as a south London side.

The Gunners were originally based at the Woolwich ordnance factory – hence "the Arsenal" – and played on Plumstead common.

By 1913 the club was in deep trouble, having achieved little. They had fallen into debt and, after finishing bottom of the First Division, attendances also dropped.

Chairman Henry Norris, having failed with a plan to merge with his previous club Fulham, decided to take Woolwich Arsenal north of the Thames with a proposed relocation to Highbury in 1913.

A mighty row broke out with Spurs and Leyton Orient, who objected to another side moving in on their territory, but there was little they could do and Arsenal duly moved into Highbury.

Former Spurs player Herbert Chapman

Relations soured even more after the infamous incident in 1919, when Norris ensured that Arsenal were voted into the restructured First Division in place of Spurs despite finishing fifth in the Second Division – below Tottenham.

The enmity was well and truly established, and not helped by the fact that it was a former Tottenham player, Herbert Chapman, who built Arsenal into a successful side between the wars while Spurs won nothing between 1921 and 1951.

But Chapman's switch was a rare one. For two clubs so close together, with just two miles of the Seven Sisters Road separating their grounds, there has been remarkably little movement between them. Few players have enjoyed successful spells with both clubs, with the exception of Pat Jennings who won FA

Cup winners' medals with both Spurs and Arsenal. In total only ten players have played for both sides.

Only one man, Terry Neill, has managed both clubs and he had considerably more success at Highbury. Joe Hulme made the opposite move to Chapman by managing Spurs after playing for Arsenal.

While other cities have their derbies, few match the intensity of this one. Liverpool and Everton are enemies on the field, of course, but their supporters are more likely to be bound together by city loyalty against a common enemy.

Spurs and Arsenal have little sympathy for each other. No wonder Spurs fans took such delight when their former midfielder Nayim scored a sensational last-minute volley from the halfway line to sink Arsenal in the 1995 European Cup-winners' Cup final.

And Arsenal supporters were celebrating long and loud when their side equalled Tottenham's feat of winning the League and Cup double by wrapping up the championship with a 1–0 win at White Hart Lane in 1971.

Arsenal's high points have included a 5–0 win at White Hart Lane in 1978, but Spurs got revenge five years later by beating their bitter rivals by the same score.

Other notable results include their meeting in the 1991 FA Cup semi-final, when a Paul Gascoigne-inspired Spurs sank Arsenal at Wembley against all odds to end the Gunners' dreams of a second double.

Pat Jennings was one of a handful of players to be successful with both north London clubs

That 3–1 win was avenged two years later when Arsenal beat Spurs 1–0 in the semi-final, also played at Wembley because of the incredible demand for tickets.

Other cup clashes have included the 1968 and 1987 League Cup semi-finals, both of which were won by Arsenal.

The record between the sides is remarkably close over the years, with Arsenal two wins and nine goals ahead in all games.

The full results to the end of 1996–97 are as follows:

	P	W	D	L	For	Ag
LEAGUE						
SPURS	120	44	28	48	168	178
ARSENAL	120	48	28	44	176	168
FA CUP						
SPURS	4	2	0	2	4	5
ARSENAL	4	2	0	2	5	4
LEAGUE CUP						
SPURS	7	2	1	4	6	8
ARSENAL	7	4	1	2	8	6
FRIENDLIES (*includes war-time games)						
SPURS	109	47	19	43	179	177
ARSENAL	109	43	19	47	177	179
CHARITY SHIELD						
SPURS	1	0	1	0	0	0
ARSENAL	1	0	1	0	0	0
TOTAL						
SPURS	241	95	49	97	357	366
ARSENAL	241	97	49	95	366	357

12 December 1992
FA Premier League
TOTTENHAM HOTSPUR 1
ARSENAL 0

This was the first meeting between the clubs in the new Premiership, and it was first blood to Tottenham.

To win any league game and keep a clean sheet is cause for celebration, but to do so over your most bitter enemies is even better.

There was plenty of striking talent on view with Teddy Sheringham playing his first north London derby alongside Gordon Durie for Spurs, while Ian Wright lined up with Kevin Campbell and Paul Merson for Arsenal.

But it was Paul Allen who settled the 231st meeting between the sides when he scored the game's only goal, running half the length of the field to pick up a return pass and slide the ball past David Seaman midway though the first half.

Allen was often an unsung hero at White Hart Lane, but fans appreciated his honest endeavour and he went into Spurs folklore after scoring the winner against Arsenal.

The other major talking point after the game was an incident between Ian Wright and David Howells, when the Arsenal striker aimed a punch at his opponent.

Although the referee missed it, television cameras picked up the offence and Wright was subsequently

banned for three games. Arsenal manager George Graham also incurred the FA's displeasure after criticising the referee, which earned him a £500 fine.

Spurs went into the match on the back of defeats by Nottingham Forest and Chelsea in successive games, but took the match to Arsenal from the start.

Allen's goal was ultimately the decider, but Arsenal gained revenge four months later when they won their FA Cup semi-final against Spurs 1–0 at Wembley, Tony Adams scoring a late winner to make up for their defeat at the same stage two years earlier.

The week before the cup final, however, Spurs were determined to end the season on a high note and won 3–1 at Highbury, with reserve striker John Hendry scoring twice and Teddy Sheringham getting the other to complete a rare double over the old enemy.

TOTTENHAM 1 ARSENAL 0 (ht 1 – 0)

Att: 33,709
Tottenham: Thorstvedt, Austin, Mabbutt, Ruddock, Edinburgh, Allen, Samways, Howells, Nayim, Durie (Barmby), Sheringham.
Arsenal: Seaman, Lyderson, Winterburn, Hillier, Bould, Adams, Jensen (Limpar), Wright, Campbell, Merson, Parlour.
Spurs' Goalscorer: Allen

2 January 1995
FA Premier League
TOTTENHAM HOTSPUR 1
ARSENAL 0

Gerry Francis' first north London derby was an unqualified success. Having taken over from Ossie Ardiles when Spurs were struggling at the wrong end of the table, the former QPR manager had led them back into the top half of the table with an unbeaten run of eight games, the last four of which had seen the defence keep clean sheets.

He had inherited world-class players in Jürgen Klinsmann, Teddy Sheringham, Darren Anderton and Gica Popescu, and it was the Romanian midfielder who scored the decisive goal after 21 minutes.

Dean Austin and David Howells combined to set Anderton free down the right and when he drove in a low cross from the right, Popescu was there to side-foot the ball home from eight yards.

It was a particularly fierce game, and a shock for

Spurs' Paul Miller attempts to stop Paul Davis in a typical blood-and-thunder derby in the early 1980s

foreign players such as Klinsmann and Ronny Rosenthal. Klinsmann had played in the fierce Milan derby for Inter but admitted that nothing came near the white-hot intensity of the north London version. "I could really sense the added tension in the air because people were stopping me in the streets and saying 'Just do us one favour and beat Arsenal'", he said.

Israeli international Rosenthal played in the Merseyside derby for Liverpool, but had never experienced anything like the atmosphere in this game.

"The Liverpool v Everton game is known as the friendly derby and often you will find supporters of both clubs within the same family, travelling to and from the game together", he said.

"In north London the rivalry carries onto the pitch. Many of the players from the two clubs know each other but once the whistle blows there are no friendships until the game ends."

Lee Dixon had the Gunners' best chance after 52 minutes when he ran onto a Stefan Schwarz pass and blasted in a powerful shot that Ian Walker saved brilliantly.

With only 14 minutes to go Klinsmann should have doubled the score when he fired a spectacular half volley wide of the post. Tempers flared after Schwarz committed a violent studs-up foul on Howells, Tottenham's man of the match, and the Swedish midfielder was finally sent off five minutes from the end for tripping Klinsmann as he ran towards goal.

Spurs held on to win with another clean sheet and Klinsmann reflected afterwards: "It is like when Inter Milan play AC Milan. You could change your whole season on the result of that one game.

"If you win that game then the whole year is fine – even if you finish 10th in the table!"

TOTTENHAM 1 ARENAL 0 (ht 1 – 0)
Att: 28,747
Tottenham: Walker, Austin, Calderwood, Mabbutt, Campbell, Anderton, Popescu (Nethercott), Howells, Rosenthal, Sheringham, Klinsmann.
Arsenal: Seaman, Dixon, Bould, Adams, Winterburn, Merson, Keown, Schwarz, Helder (Parlour), Wright, Hartson.
Spurs' Goalscorer: Popescu

The most memorable goal in the long history of meetings between the two sides was Paul Gascoigne's stunning free-kick in the 1991 FA Cup semi-final

29 April 1995
FA Premier League
ARSENAL 1
TOTTENHAM HOTSPUR 1

This game had been billed as the battle of the big guns – Klinsmann squaring up to Wright in a contest to see who was the best in north London. Both were on fire at the time and were among the two best strikers in the Premiership.

By the time of this Highbury clash, Wright had a slight edge on his rival in the goal-scoring charts, having scored 29 goals to Klinsmann's 27. In the end it was honours shared, with each man on target and the points shared one-apiece.

Having been comprehensively beaten three months earlier at White Hart Lane, Arsenal were up for revenge and started stronger. It took all of Ian Walker's brilliance in the Spurs goal to deny Wright twice in the opening 20 minutes, first with a saving tackle and then with a fingertip save at full stretch.

But for all their pressure, the Gunners didn't create too many clear cut chances and the best chance of the first half fell to Tottenham when Teddy Sheringham headed Darren Anderton's corner against the crossbar.

Arsenal started the second half stronger and regained the initiative, taking the lead shortly after the break when Wright scored from the penalty spot after Justin Edinburgh was judged to have pulled him back.

But Klinsmann was not to be outdone and the striker headed home a superb header from Edinburgh's cross to level the match in the 74th minute.

TOTTENHAM 1
ARSENAL 1 (ht 0 – 0)

Att:
38,377

Tottenham:
Walker, Austin, Calderwood, Mabbutt, Campbell, Fox, Dozzell, Howells, Rosenthal (McMahon), Sheringham, Armstrong.

Arsenal:
Seaman, Dixon, Bould, Adams, Winterburn, Merson, PLatt, Keown, Helder (Hillier), Bergkamp, Hartson.

Spurs' Goalscorer:
Kilnsmann

Jürgen Klinsmann celebrating his goal against the old enemy in April 1995

Arsenal went all out in search of the winner, but it was Spurs who could have snatched victory in the end when Sheringham had a free header at the far post, but he nodded over and the chance was lost.

Seaman also played his part in denying Spurs when he brilliantly tipped over a Rosenthal shot in the dying moments.

It had been a fine performance and one from which Spurs probably deserved more than they got.

Gerry Francis was pleased afterwards and was quick to acknowledge the contribution of Klinsmann. "The supporters appreciate Jürgen's workrate and unselfish approach and that has rubbed off on the rest of the team".

18 November 1995
FA Premier League
TOTTENHAM HOTSPUR 2
ARSENAL 1

Both sides had record signings playing in their first north London derby when the teams met at White Hart Lane in November 1995. For Spurs, Chris Armstrong had arrived from Crystal Palace for £4.5 million to fill the gap left by Jurgen Klinsmann's departure, while Arsenal's new manager Bruce Rioch had splashed out £7.5 million on Dutch striker Dennis Bergkamp.

Both knew that the north London derby wasn't like any other, and Armstrong admitted: "A lot of fans said to me that Arsenal was the game everybody wanted to win. Some fans didn't care what happened as long as we beat them.

"I arrived for my first derby a bit earlier than usual, but already the traffic was building up and there were a lot of people around – you could sense there was a different atmosphere.

"In the ground before kick-off the crowd was making a lot of noise and it gives you a real lift, especially knowing what a big game it is."

Things didn't start well for Spurs, however, as the Gunners dominated the opening stages and took the lead in the 14th minute when Bergkamp fired home from Paul Merson's pass.

But Spurs got on top and Teddy Sheringham equalised in the 29th minute from a move that he had started in his own penalty area. He headed the ball down for Jason Dozzell to volley upfield to Chris Armstrong, who set Ruel Fox on his way.

A rare show of unity, after the two sides shared the 1991 FA Charity Shield

Fox, recently signed from Newcastle, made an instant impression on the home fans with a dazzling display that left Nigel Winterburn bemused. His cross found Sheringham, who had sprinted upfield and ended the move with a diving header that David Seaman couldn't keep out.

But the winner was reserved for Armstrong, who thoroughly deserved it. He had taken a long time to start scoring after the unenviable task of replacing Klinsmann, but was running into a rich vein of form, and his confidence showed as he struck in the 54th minute.

Armstrong played a one-two with Sheringham and turned on the return pass before skipping past Steve Bould's attempted challenge to drive the ball home low past Seaman.

Both goalkeepers made great saves in the closing stages as Spurs held on for a famous win. And it was also comforting to see the partnership between Sheringham and Armstrong bearing fruit after the prophets of doom and gloom had forecast nothing but misery following the departure of Klinsmann.

As Gerry Francis said: "The partnership of Teddy and Chris more than compares with that between Teddy and Jurgen".

**TOTTENHAM 2
ARSENAL 1 (ht 1 – 1)**

Att:
38,377

Tottenham:
Walker, Austin, Calderwood, Mabbutt, Campbell, Fox, Dozzell, Howells, Rosenthal (McMahon), Sheringham, Armstrong.

Arsenal:
Seaman, Dixon, Bould, Adams, Winterburn, Merson, Platt, Keown, Helder (Hillier), Bergkamp, Hartson.

Spurs' Goalscorers:
Sheringham, Armstrong

Chapter 12

The Records

Year-by-year statistics

Season 1992–93

FA CUP

Date	Team	Venue	Att	Score	Scorer
3rd Round					
Jan 2	Marlow	A	26,636	5-1	Sheringham, Barmby, 2, Samways, 2
4th Round					
Jan 24	Norwich	A	15,003	2-0	Sheringham, 2
5th Round					
Feb 14	Wimbledon	H	26,529	3-2	Barmby, Sheringham, Anderton
6th Round					
Mar 7	Man City	A	34,050	4-2	Nayim, 3, Sedgley
Semi-final					
Apr 4	Arsenal	Wembley	76,263	0-1	

COCA-COLA CUP

Date	Team	Venue	Att	Score	Scorer
2nd Round					
1st Leg Sep 21	Brentford	H	19,365	3-1	Sheringham, Watson, Durie
2nd Leg Oct 7	Brentford	A	11,445	4-2	Anderton, Sheringham 2, Turner
3rd Round					
Oct 28	Man City	A	18,399	1-0	Samways
4th Round					
Dec 2	Nottingham F	A	22,312	0-2	

PLAYER APPEARANCES

Name	Lge	(Sub)	Gls	Cup	(Sub)	Gls
Allen P	38	x	3	9	x	x
Anderton D	34	(2)	6	7	(1)	2
Austin D	34	(1)	x	8	(1)	x
Barmby N	22	(5)	6	7	(2)	3
Bergsson G	5	(5)	x	x	(1)	x
Campbell S	1	(1)	1	x	x	x
Cundy J	15	(2)	1	2	x	x
Dearden K	1	(1)	x	x	x	x
Durie G	17	x	3	3	x	1
Edinburgh J	32	(1)	x	9	(1)	x
Fenwick T	5	(2)	x	x	x	x
Gray A	17	(8)	1	x	x	x
Hendry J	5	(2)	2	x	x	x
Hill D	4	(2)	x	x	x	x
Hodges L	4	(4)	x	x	x	x
Howells D	18	(2)	1	4	(2)	x
Mabbutt G	29	x	2	7	x	x
McDonald D	2	x	x	x	x	x
Moran P	3	(3)	x	x	x	x
Nayim	x	18	(3)	3	(5)	3
Nethercott S	5	(2)	x	x	x	x
Ruddock N	38	x	(3)	9	x	x
Samways V	34	x	x	8	(3)	x
Sedgley S	22	(2)	3	5	(1)	x
Sheringham E	38	x	21	9	x	7
Thorstvedt E	27	(2)	x	7	x	x
Turner A	18	(11)	3	x	(3)	1
Tuttle D	5	(1)	x	2	x	x
Van den Hauwe P	18	(5)	x	2	x	
Walker I	17	x	x	2	x	x
Watson K	5	(1)	x	x	(2)	x
OWN GOAL	1					

	PREMIERSHIP					
Date	**Team**	**Venue**	**Att**	**Score**	**Position**	**Scorer**
Aug 15	Southampton	A	19,654	0-0		
Aug 19	Coventry	H	24,388	0-2		
Aug 22	Crystal P	H	25,237	2-2	18	Durie, Sedgley
Aug 25	Leeds Utd	A	28,218	0-5		
Aug 30	Ipswich	A	20,100	1-1		Cundy
Sep 2	Sheffield U	H	21,332	2-0		Sheringham, Durie
Sep 5	Everton	H	26,503	2-1	15	Allen, Turner
Sep 14	Coventry	A	15,348	0-1		
Sep 19	Man Utd	H	33,296	1-1	14	Durie
Sep 27	Sheffield W	A	24,895	0-2		
Oct 3	QPR	A	19,845	1-4	19	Sheringham
Oct 17	M'brough	H	24,735	2-2	19	Sheringham, Barmby
Oct 25	Wimbledon	A	8,628	1-1		Barmby
Oct 31	Liverpool	H	32,917	2-0	17	Nayim, Ruddock
Nov 7	Blackburn R	A	17,305	2-0	14	Howells, Sheringham
Nov 21	Aston Villa	H	32,852	0-0	15	
Nov 28	Man City	A	25,496	1-0	12	Phelan, (og)
Dec 5	Chelsea	H	31,540	1-2	14	Campbell
Dec 12	Arsenal	H	33,709	1-0	13	Allen
Dec 19	Oldham	A	11,735	1-2	13	Sheringham
Dec 26	Norwich	A	19,413	0-0	13	
Dec 28	Nottingham F	H	32,118	2-1	12	Barmby, Mabbutt
Jan 9	Man Utd	A	35,648	1-4	12	Barmby
Jan 16	Sheffield W	H	25,702	0-2	14	
Jan 27	Ipswich	H	23,738	0-2		
Jan 30	Crystal P	A	20,937	3-1	13	Sheringham, 2, Gray
Feb 7	Southampton	H	20,098	4-2		Sheringham, 2, Barmby, Anderton
Feb 10	Everton	A	16,164	2-1		Mabbutt, Allen
Feb 20	Leeds Utd	H	32,040	4-0	9	Sheringham, 3, Ruddock
Feb 27	QPR	H	32,341	3-2	8	Sheringham, 2, Anderton
Mar 2	Sheffield U	A	16,654	0-6		
Mar 10	Aston Villa	A	37,727	0-0		
Mar 20	Chelsea	A	25,157	1-1	11	Sheringham
Mar 24	Man City	H	27,247	3-1		Anderton, Nayim, Turner
Apr 9,	Norwich	H	31,425	5-1		Ruddock, Sheringham, 2, Barmby, Nayim
Apr 12	Nottingham F	A	25,682	1-2	9	Sedgley
Apr 17	Oldham	H	26,663	4-1	6	Sheringham, 2, Anderton, Turner
Apr 20	M'brough	A	14,472	0-3		
May 1	Wimbledon	H	24,473	1-1	9	Anderton
May 5	Blackburn R	H	23,097	1-2		Anderton
May 8	Liverpool	A	43,385	2-6	11	Sheringham, Sedgley
May 11	Arsenal	A	26,393	3-1		Sheringham, Hendry, 2

FINAL LEAGUE POSITION – 8th

Season 1993–94

PREMIERSHIP						
Date	**Team**	**Venue**	**Att**	**Score**	**Position**	**Scorer**
Aug 14	Newcastle Utd	A	34,565	1-0		Sheringham
Aug 16	Arsenal	H	28,355	0-1		
Aug 21	Man City	H	24,535	1-0	8	Sedgley
Aug 25	Liverpool	A	42,456	2-1		Sheringham, 2
Aug 28	Aston Villa	A	32,498	0-1	9	
Sep , 1	Chelsea	H	27,567	1-1		Sheringham
Sep 11	Sheffield U	A	21,325	2-2	10	Sheringham, 2
Sep 18	Oldham	H	24,614	5-0	5	Sheringham, Durie, Sedgley, 2, Dozzell
Sep 26	Ipswich	A	19,437	2-2		Sheringham, Dozzell
Oct 3	Everton	H	27,487	3-2		Sheringham, Anderton, Caskey
Oct 16	Man Utd	A	44,655	1-2	5	Caskey
Oct 23	Swindon	H	31,394	1-1	8	Dozzell
Oct 30	Blackburn R	A	17,462	0-1	10	
Nov 6	Southampton	A	16,017	0-1	11	
Nov 20	Leeds Utd	H	31,275	1-1	10	Anderton
Nov 24	Wimbledon	H	17,744	1-1		Barmby
Nov 27	QPR	A	17,694	1-1	10	Anderton
Dec 4	Newcastle Utd	H	30,780	1-2	14	Barmby
Dec 6	Arsenal	A	35,669	1-1		Anderton
Dec 11	Man City	A	21,566	2-0	11	Dozzell, 2
Dec 18	Liverpool	H	31,394	3-3	14	Samways, Hazard, Caskey
Dec 27	Norwich	H	31,130	1-3	14	Barmby
Dec 28	West Ham	A	20,787	3-1	11	Dozzell, Hazard, Anderton
Jan 1	Coventry	H	26,015	1-2	12	Caskey
Jan 3	Sheffield W	A	32,514	0-1	13	
Jan 15	Man Utd	H	31,343	0-1	15	
Jan 22	Swindon	A	16,464	1-2	15	Barmby
Feb 5	Sheffield W	H	23,078	1-3	16	Rosenthal
Feb 12	Blackburn R	H	30,236	0-2	16	
Feb 27	Chelsea	A	19,398	3-4		Sedgley, Dozzell, Gray
Mar 2	Aston Villa	H	17,452	1-1		Rosenthal
Mar 5	Sheffield U	H	25,741	2-2	16	Scott, Dozzell
Mar 19	Ipswich	H	26,653	1-1	17	Barmby
Mar 26	Everton	A	23,460	1-0	16	Sedgley
Apr 2	Norwich	A	21,181	2-1	16	Sheringham, Woodthorpe, (og)
Apr 4	West Ham	H	31,502	1-4	16	Sheringham
Apr 9	Coventry	A	14,487	0-1	18	
Apr 17	Leeds Utd	A	33,658	0-2		
Apr 23	Southampton	H	25,959	3-0	16	Sedgley, Samways, Anderton
Apr 30	Wimbledon	A	20,875	1-2	16	Sheringham
May 5	Oldham	A	14,283	2-0		Samways, Howells
May 7	QPR	H	26,105	1-2	15	Sheringham

FINAL LEAGUE POSITION – 15th

FA CUP

Date	Team	Venue	Att	Score	Scorer
3rd Round					
Jan 8	Peterborough	A	19,169	1-1	Dozzell
Jan 19	Peterborough	H	24,893	1-1	Barmby
	(Spurs won 5-4				
	on penalties)				
4th Round					
Jan 29	Ipswich	A	22,539	0-3	

COCA-COLA CUP

Date	Team	Venue	Att	Score	Scorer
2nd Round					
1st Leg					
Sep 22	Burnley	A	16,844	0-0	
2nd Leg					
Oct 6	Burnley	H	20,614	3-1	Sheringham, 2,
					Howells,
3rd Round					
Oct 27	Derby	A	19,885	1-0	Barmby
4th Round					
Dec 1	Blackburn R	H	22,295	1-0	Campbell,
5th Round					
Jan 12	Aston Villa	H	31,408	1-2	Caskey

PLAYER APPEARANCES

Name	Lge	(Sub)	Gls	Cup	(Sub)	Gls
Allen P	1	(1)	x	x	x	x
Anderton D	37	(2)	6	8	x	x
Austin D	23	(3)	x	3	(1)	x
Barmby N	27	x	5	6	x	2
Calderwood C	26	x	x	8	x	x
Campbell S	34	(7)	x	8	(2)	1
Carr S	1	x	x	1	x	x
Caskey D	25	(9)	4	7	(1)	1
Dozzell J	32	(4)	8	6	x	1
Durie G	10	x	1	2	x	x
Edinburgh J	25	(1)	x	6	x	x
Gray A	2	(2)	1	x	x	x
Hazard M	17	(4)	2	2	x	x
Hendry J	3	(3)	x	x	(2)	x
Hill D	3	(2)	x	x	x	x
Howells D	18	(3)	1	2	(1)	1
Kerslake D	17	(1)	x	5	(1)	x
Mabbutt G	29	x	x	3	x	x
Mahorn P	1	x	x	x	x	x
Moran P	5	(5)	x	x	(1)	x
Nethercott S	10	(1)	x	1	x	x
Robinson S	2	(1)	x	x	x	x
Rosenthal R	15	(4)	2	x	x	x
Samways V	39	x	3	8	x	x
Scott K	12	x	1	x	x	x
Sedgley S	42	x	6	8	x	x
Sheringham E	19	(2)	13	2	x	2
Thorstvedt E	32	x	x	5	x	x
Turner A	1	(1)	x	x	x	x
Walker I	11	(1)	x	3	x	x
OWN GOALS	1					

Sol Campbell, now the best young defender in England, made his debut as a striker against Chelsea in December 1992

Season 1994–95

					PREMIERSHIP	
Date	**Team**	**Venue**	**Att**	**Score**	**Position**	**Scorer**
Aug 20	Sheffield W	A	34,051	4-3		Sheringham, Klinsmann, Barmby, Anderton
Aug 24	Everton	H	24,553	2-1		Klinsmann, 2
Aug 27	Man Utd	H	24,502	0-1	8	
Aug 30	Ipswich	A	22,430	3-1		Klinsmann, 2, Dumitrescu
Sep 12	Southampton	H	22,387	1-2		Klinsmann
Sep 17	Leicester City	A	21,300	1-3	9	Klinsmann
Sep 24	Nottingham F	H	24,558	1-4	12	Dumitrescu
Oct 1	Wimbledon	A	16,802	2-1	10	Sheringham, Popescu
Oct 8	QPR	H	25,799	1-1	10	Barmby
Oct 15	Leeds Utd	A	39,362	1-1	12	Sheringham
Oct 22	Man City	A	25,473	2-5	13	Dumitrescu, 2
Oct 29	West Ham	H	26,271	3-1	11	Klinsmann, Sheringham, Barmby
Nov 5	Blackburn R	A	26,933	0-2	13	
Nov 19	Aston Villa	H	26,899	3-4	15	Sheringham, Klinsmann, Bosnich, (og)
Nov 23	Chelsea	H	27,037	0-0		
Nov 26	Liverpool	A	35,007	1-1	14	Ruddock, (og)
Dec 3	Newcastle Utd	H	28,002	4-2	11	Sheringham, 3, Popescu
Dec 10	Sheffield W	H	25,912	3-1	10	Barmby, Klinsmann, Calderwood
Dec 17	Everton	A	32,813	0-0	10	
Dec 26	Norwich	A	21,814	2-0	8	Barmby, Sheringham
Dec 27	Crystal P	H	27,730	0-0		
Dec 31	Coventry	A	19,965	4-0	6	Darby, (og), Barmby, Anderton, Sheringham
Jan 2	Arsenal	H	28,757	1-0	6	Popescu
Jan 14	West Ham	A	24,578	2-1	6	Sheringham, Klinsmann
Jan 25	Aston Villa	A	40,017	0-1		
Feb 5	Blackburn R	H	28,124	3-1	6	Klinsmann, Barmby, Anderton
Feb 11	Chelsea	A	38,120	1-1	6	Sheringham
Feb 25	Wimbledon	H	27,258	1-2	7	Klinsmann
Mar 4	Nottingham F	A	28,711	2-2	6	Sheringham, Calderwood
Mar 8	Ipswich	H	24,930	3-0		Klinsmann, Barmby, Youds (og)
Mar 15	Man Utd	A	43,802	0-0		
Mar 18	Leicester City	H	30,851	1-0	7	Klinsmann
Mar 22	Liverpool	H	31,988	0-0		
Apr 2	Southampton	A	15,105	3-4	7	Sheringham, 2, Klinsmann
Apr 11	Man City	H	27,410	2-1		Howells, Klinsmann
Apr 14	Crystal P	A	18,068	1-1		Klinsmann
Apr 17	Norwich C	H	32,304	1-0	7	Sheringham
Apr 29	Arsenal	A	38,377	1-1	7	Klinsmann
May 3	Newcastle Utd	A	35,603	3-3		Barmby, Klinsmann, Anderton
May 6	QPR	A	18,637	1-2	7	Sheringham
May 9	Coventry	H	24,930	1-3		Anderton
May 14	Leeds Utd	H	33,040	1-1	7	Sheringham

FINAL LEAGUE POSITION – 7th

FA CUP

Date	Team	Venue	Att	Score	Scorer
3rd Round					
Jan 7	Altrincham	H	25,057	3-0	Rosenthal, Sheringham, Nethercott
4th Round					
Jan 29	Sunderland	A	21,135	4-1	Klinsmann, 2, Mabbutt, Sheringham
5th Round					
Feb 18	Southampton	H	28,091	1-1	Klinsmann
Mar 1 Replay	Southampton	A	15,172	6-2	Rosenthal, 3, Anderton, Barmby, Sheringham
6th Round					
Mar 11	Liverpool	A	39,592	2-1	Klinsmann, Sheringham
Semi-final					
Apr 9	Everton	Elland Rd	38,226	1-4	Klinsmann

COCA-COLA CUP

Date	Team	Venue	Att	Score	Scorer
2nd Round					
1st Leg Sep 21	Watford,	A	13,659	6-3	Klinsmann, 3, Anderton, Dumitrescu, Sheringham
2nd Leg Oct 4	Watford	H	17,798	2-3	Barmby, Klinsmann
3rd Round					
Oct 26	Notts County	A	16,952	0-3	

PLAYER APPEARANCES

Name	Lge	(Sub)	Gls	Cup	(Sub)	Gls
Anderton D	37	x	5	8	x	2
Austin D	24	(1)	x	7	(1)	x
Barmby N	38	(1)	9	8	x	2
Calderwood C	36	(1)	2	7	x	x
Campbell S	30	(1)	x	6	x	x
Caskey D	4	(3)	x	1	(1)	x
Dozzell J	7	(1)	x	2	x	x
Dumitrescu I	13	(2)	4	2	x	1
Edingburgh J	31	(2)	x	6	x	x
Hazard M	11	(9)	x	2	(1)	x
Hill D	3	(2)	x	2	(2)	x
Howells D	26	x	1	8	(1)	x
Kerslake D	18	(2)	x	2	x	x
Klinsmann J	41	x	20	9	x	9
Mabbutt G	36	(3)	x	8	x	1
McMahon G	2	x	x	x	x	x
Nethercott S	17	(9)	x	4	(2)	1
Popescu G	23	x	3	5	x	x
Rosenthal R	20	(6)	x	5	(2)	4
Scott K	4	x	x	x	x	x
Sheringham E	42	(1)	18	8	x	5
Thorstvedt E	1	x	x	1	x	x
Turner A	1	x	x	x	x	x
Walker I	41	x	x	8	x	x
OWN GOALS	4					

Nick Barmby scored 11 goals in 46 games during 1994–95, his best return for Tottenham.

Season 1995–96

			PREMIERSHIP			
Date	Team	Venue	Att	Score	Position	Scorer
Aug 19,	Man City	A	30,827	1-1		Sheringham
Aug 23	Aston Villa	H	26,598	0-1		
Aug 26	Liverpool	H	31,254	1-3	19	Barnes, (og)
Aug 30	West Ham	A	23,516	1-1		Rosenthal
Sep 9	Leeds Utd	H	30,034	2-1	13	Howells, Sheringham
Sep 16	Sheffield W	A	26,565	3-1	11	Sheringham, 2, Walker
Sep 25	QPR	A	15,659	3-2		Sheringham, 2, Dozzell
Sep 30	Wimbledon	H	25,321	3-1	9	Sheringham, 2, Elkins, (og)
Oct 14	Nottingham F	H	32,876	0-1	10	
Oct 22	Everton	A	33,629	1-1	9	Armstrong
Oct 29	Newcastle Utd	H	32,257	1-1	9	Armstrong
Nov 4	Coventry	A	17,567	3-2	9	Fox, Sheringham, Howells
Nov 18	Arsenal	H	32,894	2-1	9	Sheringham, Armstrong
Nov 21	M'brough	A	29,487	1-0		Armstrong
Nov 25	Chelsea	A	31,059	0-0	5	
Dec 2	Everton	H	32,894	0-0	5	
Dec 9	QPR	H	28,851	1-0	5	Sheringham
Dec 16	Wimbledon	A	16,193	1-0	3	Fox
Dec 23	Bolton	H	30,702	2-2	4	Sheringham, Armstrong
Dec 26	Southampton	A	15,238	0-0	3	
Dec 30	Blackburn R	A	30,004	1-2	4	Sheringham
Jan 1	Man Utd	H	32,852	4-1	4	Armstrong, 2, Sheringham, Campbell
Jan 13	Man City	H	31,438	1-0	3	Armstrong
Jan 21	Aston Villa	A	35,666	1-2	4	Fox
Feb 3	Liverpool	A	40,628	0-0	5	
Feb 12	West Ham	H	29,781	0-1		
Feb 24	Sheffield W	H	32,047	1-0	5	Armstrong
Mar 2	Southampton	H	26,320	1-0	5	Dozzell
Mar 16	Blackburn R	H	31,803	2-3	7	Sheringham, Armstrong
Mar 20	Bolton W	A	17,829	3-2		Howells, Fox, Armstrong
Mar 24	Man Utd	A	50,508	0-1	6	
Mar 30	Coventry	H	26,808	3-1	6	Sheringham, Fox, 2
Apr 6	Nottingham F	A	27,053	1-2	7	Armstrong
Apr 8	M'brough	H	32,026	1-1	6	Armstrong
Apr 15	Arsenal	A	38,273	0-0		
Apr 27	Chelsea	H	32,918	1-1	8	Armstrong
May 2	Leeds Utd	A	30,024	3-1		Armstrong, Anderton, 2
May 5	Newcastle Utd	A	36,589	1-1	8	Dozzell

FINAL LEAGUE POSITION – 8th

FA CUP

Date	Team	Venue	Att	Score	Scorer
3rd Round					
Jan 6	Hereford Utd	A	8,806	1-1	Rosenthal
Jan 17	Hereford Utd	H	31,304	5-1	Sheringham, 3, Armstrong, 2
4th Round					
Jan 27	Wolves	H	32,812	1-1	Wilson
Feb 7	Wolves	A	27,846	2-0	Rosenthal, Sheringham
5th Round					
Feb 19	Nottingham F	A	17,009		(Match abandoned due to snow)
Feb 28,	Nottingham F	A	18,600	2-2	Armstrong, 2
Mar 9	Nottingham F	H	31,055	1-1	Sheringham
(Tottenham, lost, 3-1, on, penalties)					

COCA-COLA CUP

Date	Team	Venue	Att	Score	Scorer
2nd Round					
1st Leg Sep 20	Chester City	H	17,645	4-0	Rosenthal, Sheringham, Armstrong, 2
2nd Leg Oct 4	Chester City	A	5,372	3-1	Sheringham, 2, Howells
3rd Round					
Oct 25	Coventry City	A	18,227	2-3	Armstrong, Busst, (og)

PLAYER APPEARANCES

Name	Lge	(Sub)	Gls	Cup	(Sub)	Gls
Anderton D	8	(2)	2	1	x	x
Armstrong C	36	x	15	9	x	7
Austin D	28	x	x	7	x	x
Calderwood C	29	(3)	x	7	x	x
Campbell S	31	x	1	8	x	x
Caskey D	3	x	x	3	x	x
Cundy J	1	(1)	x	x	x	x
Dozzell J	28	(4)	3	6	(3)	x
Dumitrescu I	5	x	x	x	x	x
Edinburgh J	22	(7)	x	6	(1)	x
Fox R	26	x	6	6	x	x
Howells D	29	x	3	4	1	x
Kerslake D	2	x	x	x	x	x
Mabbutt G	32	x	x	9	x	x
McMahon G	14	(7)	x	4	(1)	x
Nethercott S	13	(4)	x	3	(1)	x
Rosenthal R	33	(7)	1	7	3	x
Scott K	2	(2)	x	1	(1)	x
Sheringham E	38	x	16	9	x	8
Sinton A	9	(1)	x	x	x	x
Slade S	5	(4)	x	3	(3)	x
Walker I	38	x	x	9	x	x
Wilson C	28	x	x	8	(1)	1
OWN GOALS	3					

After a slow start, Chris Armstrong scored 22 goals in 45 games during his first season at White Hart Lane

Season 1996–97

				PREMIERSHIP			
Date	Team	Venue	Att	Score	Position	Scorer	
Aug 17	Blackburn R	A	26,960	2-0	6	Armstrong, 2	
Aug 21	Derby County	H	28,219	1-1	6	Sheringham	
Aug 24	Everton	H	29,696	0-0	8		
Sep 4	Wimbledon	A	17,506	0-1	12		
Sep 7	Newcastle Utd	H	32,525	1-2	13	Allen	
Sep 14	Southampton	A	15,251	1-0	11	Armstrong	
Sep 22	Leicester City	H	24,159	1-2	12	Wilson	
Sep 29	Man Utd	A	54,943	0-2	14		
Oct 12	Aston Villa	H	32,847	1-0	11	Nielsen	
Oct 19	M'brough	A	30,215	3-0	8	Sheringham, 2, Fox	
Oct 26	Chelsea	A	28,373	1-3	9	Armstrong	
Nov 2	West Ham	H	32,999	1-0	8	Armstrong	
Nov 16	Sunderland	H	31,867	2-0	7	Sinton, Sheringham	
Nov 24	Arsenal	A	38,264	1-3	9	Sinton	
Dec , 2	Liverpool	H	32,899	0-2	11		
Dec 7	Coventry	A	19,675	2-1	10	Sheringham, Sinton	
Dec 14	Leeds Utd	A	33,783	0-0	9		
Dec 21	Sheffield W	H	30,996	1-1	10	Nielsen	
Dec 26	Southampton	H	30,549	3-1	8	Nielsen, Iversen, 2	
Dec 28	Newcastle Utd	A	36,308	1-7	10	Nielsen	
Jan 12	Man Utd	H	33,026	1-2	10	Allen	
Jan 19	Nottingham F	A	27,303	1-2	10	Sinton	
Jan 29	Blackburn R	H	22,943	2-1	9	Iversen, Sinton	
Feb 1	Chelsea	H	33,027	1-2	10	Howells	
Feb 15	Arsenal	H	33,039	0-0	9		
Feb 24	West Ham	A	23,998	3-4	11	Howells, Anderton, Sheringham	
Mar 1	Nottingham F	H	32,805	0-1	13		
Mar 4	Sunderland	A	20,785	4-0	10	Iversen, 3, Nielsen	
Mar 15	Leeds Utd	H	33,040	1-0	10	Anderton	
Mar 19	Leicester City	A	20,593	1-1	10	Sheringham	
Mar 22	Derby County	A	18,083	2-4	10	Dozzell, Wilson	
Apr 5	Wimbledon	H	32,654	1-0	9	Dozzell	
Apr 9	Sheffield W	A	22,667	1-2	9	Nielsen	
Apr 12	Everton	A	36,380	0-1	9		
Apr 19	Aston Villa	A	39,339	1-1	9	Vega	
Apr 24	M'brough	H	29,940	1-0	9	Sinton	
May 3	Liverpool	A	40,003	1-2	9	Anderton	
May11	Coventry	H	32,029	1-2	10	McVeigh	

FINAL LEAGUE POSITION – 10th

FA CUP

Date	Team	Venue	Att	Score	Scorer
3rd Round					
Jan 5	Man Utd	A	52,495	0-2	

COCA-COLA CUP

Date	Team	Venue	Att	Score	Scorer
2nd Round					
1st Leg Sep 17	Preston NE	A	16,258	1-1	Anderton
2nd Leg Sep 25	Preston NE	H	20,080	3-0	Allen, 2, Anderton
Oct 23	Sunderland	H	24,867	2-1	Armstrong, Campbell
3rd Round					
Nov 27	Bolton W	A	18,621	6-1	Sheringham

PLAYER APPEARANCES 1996–97

Name	Lge	(Sub)	Gls	Cup	(Sub)	Gls
Allen R	12	(3)	2	4	(1)	2
Anderton D	16	(2)	3	3	x	2
Armstrong C	12	x	5	3	x	1
Austin D	15	(2)	1	x	x	x
Baardsen E	2	(1)	x	x	x	x
Carr S	26	(2)	x	4	x	x
Calderwood C	34	x	x	5	x	x
Campbell S	38	x	x	5	x	1
Clapham J	17	(1)	x	x	x	x
Dozzell J	10	(7)	2	1	x	x
Edinburgh J	24	(3)	x	3	x	x
Fenn N	4	(4)	x	1	x	x
Howells D	32	x	2	5	x	x
Iversen S	16	x	6	x	x	x
Mabbutt G	1	x	x	x	x	x
McVeigh P	3	(1)	1	x	x	x
Nethercott S	9	(7)	x	x	x	x
Nielsen A	29	(1)	6	4	(1)	x
Fox R	25	(6)	1	4	(1)	x
Rosenthal R	20	(16)	1	x	x	x
Scales J	12	(2)	x	x	x	x
Sheringham E	29	x	7	3	1	x
Sinton A	33	(1)	6	3	x	x
Walker I	37	x	x	5	x	x
Wilson C	26	(3)	1	4	x	x
Vega R	8	x	1	x	x	x

England defender Sol Campbell was the only ever-present player during an injury-hit 1996–97 season. He was also Tottenham's Player of the Year

Miscellaneous Premiership records

The name of Tottenham Hotspur FC is synonymous with record-breaking excellence. Here we present some of the facts and figures that have emerged from the Premiership years. NB – these are Premier League statistics only

Team Records

OVERALL RECORD

P	W	D	L	F	A	Pts
202	70	63	69	274	272	273

Win ratio of 34.7%
Defeat ratio of 34.0%
Strike-rate ratio of 1.36 goals per game

HOME RECORD

P	W	D	L	F	A	Pts
101	41	32	28	146	118	155

Win ratio of 41%
Defeat ratio of 32%
Strike-rate ratio of 1.46 goals per game

AWAY RECORD

P	W	D	L	F	A	Pts
101	29	31	41	128	154	118

Win ratio of 29%
Defeat ratio of 41%
Strike-rate ratio of 1.28 goals per game

HIGHS AND LOWS

Biggest victory

5–0 vs. Oldham, 1993–94

Heaviest defeats

7–1 vs. Newcastle United 1996–97
6–0 vs. Sheffield United 1992–93

Biggest away victory

4–0 vs. Coventry City 1994–95
4–0 vs. Sunderland 1996–97

Heaviest home defeat

4–1 vs. West Ham 1993–94
4–1 vs. Nottingham Forest 1994–95

Fewest points

45 in season 1993–94 (finished 15th)

Most goals for

66 in season 1994–95

Fewest goals for

44 in season 1996–97

Most goals against

66 in season 1992–93

Fewest goals against

38 in season 1995–96

Most victories

16 in seasons 1992–93, 1994–95, 1995–96

Fewest wins

11 in season 1993–94

Fewest defeats

9 in season 1995–96

Most defeats

19 in season 1993–94

Most draws

14 in season 1994–95

Teddy Sheringham, Spurs' record Premiership scorer

SEQUENCES AND TOTALS

Unbeaten sequence at home

7 games in season 1993–93 (twice) and 1995–96

Most home wins in a season

11 games in season 1992–93

Longest run without a home win in a season

14 games in season 1993–94

Most home defeats in a season

9 games in season 1993–94

Most away wins in a season

7 games in season 1993–94 and 1995–96

Most away defeats in a season

11 games in season 1996–97

Longest unbeaten run

10 games from 23 November 1994 to 14 January 1995

Longest run without a victory

10 games in season 1993–94

Worst run of results

One win between 12 December 1993 and 26 March 1994

Most victories in a row

5 games in season 1992–93

Most home victories in a row

6 games in season 1992–93

Most away victories in a row

3 games in seasons 1994–95 and 1995–96

Most defeats in a row

7 games in season 1993–94

ATTENDANCES

Highest home attendance

33,709 vs. Arsenal in season 1992-93

Highest away attendance

54,943 vs. Manchester United in season 1996-97

Individual Records

GOALSCORING

Best scoring in a season

21 goals by Teddy Sheringham in season 1992–93

Highest scorer (Premier League only)

Teddy Sheringham 75 goals (1992 to 1997)

Top scorers per season

21 goals by Sheringham in season 1992–93

14 goals by Sheringham in season 1993–94

20 goals by Klinsmann in season 1994–95

16 goals by Sheringham in season 1995–96

7 goals by Sheringham in season 1996–97

Top five aggregate goalscorers (all-time)

1 Jimmy Greaves 220 goals

2 Bobby Smith 176 goals

3 Cliff Jones 135 goals

4 George Hunt 124 goals

5 Martin Chivers 118 goals

Most hat-tricks

2 by Teddy Sheringham

ATTENDANCES

Longest run of appearances

104 consecutive appearances by Ian Walker between November 1994 and May 1997

Top five aggregate appearances (all-time)

1 Steve Perryman 655 appearances

2 Pat Jennings 472 appearances

3 Gary Mabbutt 466 appearances

4 Ted Ditchburn 418 appearances

5 Cyril Knowles 401 appearances

Index

Acknowledgements

The publishers would like to thank the following sources for their kind permission to reproduce the pictures in this book:

All Action/Duncan Raban; Allsport UK Ltd./Clive Brunskill, David Cannon, Graham Chadwick, Chris Cole, Stu Forster, Mike Hewitt, Ross Kinnard, Steve Morton, Gary M. Prior, Ben Radford, Mark Thompson, Anton Want; Allsport Historical Collection; Colorsport; Empics/Laurence Griffiths,

Aubrey Washington; Hulton Getty; Mark Leech; Popperfoto; Professional Sport/Corey Ross; Sport & General Press Agency.

Every effort has been made to acknowledge correctly and contact the source and/copyright holder of each picture, and Carlton Books Limited apologises for any unintentional errors or omissions which will be corrected in future editions of this book.